The Journey Continues

by
Helen Edds Frazier

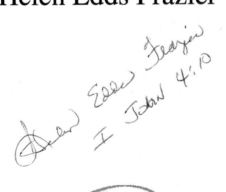

Helen Edds Frazier
I John 4:10

xulon PRESS

Copyright © 2004 by Helen Edds Frazier

The Journey Continues
by Helen Edds Frazier

Printed in the United States of America

ISBN 1-594677-79-4

Bible quotations are taken from the King James version of the Bible.

www.xulonpress.com

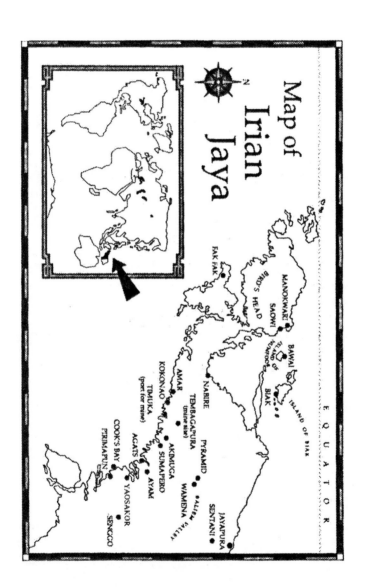

Map of Irian Jaya

Dedication

This book is lovingly dedicated to my
husband Bob,
without whose support and encouragement
(and perhaps a little shove)
it might never have been written.

My thanks go to him for enduring extra
household dust,
helping with meals and in many other ways,
so that I could squeeze in time to write.

Preface

To the question, "Is this an autobiography?" technically the answer would have to be "yes." But realistically, it is not intended as a story about myself. It is a story of God in action.

Fortunately, I kept a journal for close to 40 years, providing details that I probably could not have remembered so precisely otherwise. These notes supplied fuel for a lot of what I have shared in this book. Unfortunately, I did not manage to record everything. God did so much more than is told in these pages.

My husband Bob has graciously given me permission to include some information from his book, *"Our Passionate Journey,"* which was first published in 1994.

We both feel blessed that God has given us such full lives and so many unique experiences. Admittedly some have been very difficult, but there has also been much joy and God has been with us all the way. His presence and help are not only for us, but for anyone who will seek a personal relationship with Him. We hope that what we have shared will honor Him and encourage you.

Foreword

The God of creation and salvation has commissioned His followers to go into all the world and preach the gospel. We refer to those who respond to God's call as "missionaries." Missionary life can be exciting, demanding and sometimes dangerous.

Helen Edds Frazier responded to God's call and went to Zimbabwe, Africa, a country of great need and also one that faced many problems. A large rebel group did all possible to overthrow the government. The situation eventually grew so serious that the mission had to evacuate its workers at TEAM's hospital.

From Zimbabwe, Helen moved on to a very primitive and isolated part of the world, Irian Jaya, now called Papua. Numerous tribes inhabit that land, of whom many were head hunters and cannibals. The first two TEAM missionaries to go to Papua were killed by native tribesmen.

I wondered if any missionaries would go to that needy, dangerous land. Several did, one of whom was Helen Frazier. Their faithful ministry resulted in many coming to know the Lord Jesus as Saviour. I had an opportunity to visit the field, and was excited to see many churches along the coast and in the mountain areas.

I'm glad Helen has written this book and know that the readers will find it very interesting, as it gives an insight of what God can do through His faithful servants – the missionaries.

Delbert A. Kuehl
Former TEAM Missionary to Japan
and Candidate Secretary

Table of Contents

SHOCK

Chapter 1

Feelings of shock, confusion and disbelief even greater than feelings of terror swept over me! Screams for help quickly changed to cries of "*Tolong*" and "*Polisi*," i.e., "help" and "police" in the Indonesian language, as I remembered that no one who might hear me spoke English.

A missionary with TEAM (The Evangelical Alliance Mission), an interdenominational faith based mission with international headquarters in Wheaton, Illinois, I was in my third term of overseas service – first in Rhodesia (currently Zimbabwe), Africa, and now twice in Irian Jaya, Indonesia, (formerly known as Dutch New Guinea, later as West Irian, then as Irian Jaya and now as Papua). Today was the first day of my new assignment at the field headquarters in Manokwari. Manokwari, a small town on the north coast, is in an area called "the Bird's Head." The western half of the island, where TEAM works, simulates the shape of a bird in flight.

Thus the north coast acquired this descriptive label.

The day was hot that August afternoon with its usual tropical temperature and humidity, and for me the heat was intensified a little by my low grade fever from a lingering tropical illness. The second-floor windows were open to draw in every bit of fresh air available.

The two-story building was quiet. Minutes earlier field chairman Ron Hill and his wife Charlene, the field bookkeeper, had closed the mission headquarters office on the ground floor below and headed home for lunch. In my small apartment on the second floor, I had started preparing lunch for myself.

Then, as I had walked from my kitchen into the adjoining living room, my assailant — an Irianese man — suddenly stepped out from his hiding place, quickly locking both of my wrists in his grip! Like an animal crouching to spring on its prey, he had flattened himself against the wall between the kitchen and living room and waited for me to walk through the doorway. Now he held both of my wrists in a viselike grip that felt almost superhuman in strength. I could not extract myself.

Just as quickly as he had grasped my wrists, he swept me into his arms and carried me into the apartment's tiny bathroom. Attempts to free myself were futile as he forced me down onto the bathroom floor and positioned my head so that it was wedged into a small space between the wall and a pipe beneath the sink. Clearly, he had thought this through ahead of time. Somehow, subconsciously at least, I had assumed that things like this did not happen to missionaries. Martyrdom and suffering for Christ – possibly yes. But senseless rape – no!

The stark reality was that the building remained quiet; there was no response to my cries for help, and I could not free myself! Delay seemed the only remaining avenue of possible escape. He covered my mouth with one of his strong hands to keep me from screaming for help, but when he removed it I began to talk. I talked at length, as calmly as possible, saying anything I could think of – asking for a drink of water, asking to move to a more comfortable place – anything to gain time. I sought to appeal to any sense of compassion the man might have and also prayed aloud in the Indonesian language. An employee of the mission, Piet (pronounced Pete) was expected to protect me, not harm me. Covering my face with wet kisses, he told me that he loved me and wanted to marry me. I contended that if he really loved me, he would not hurt me.

An hour or so passed. Having fought until my strength was completely gone and words provided no further delay, I lay limp on the floor thinking, *"What an ugly way to die!"*

Incredibly, at that very instant God's voice came, not audibly, but very clearly: *"You are not going to die now!"*

As unlikely as it appeared at that moment, God was with me. My journey with Him was not even close to being finished. He who had given me life had more life ahead!

LIFE

Chapter 2

It was on a Tuesday evening in September of 1934 that I entered the world via my maternal grandmother's home in the small town of Fort Smith, Arkansas. My mother, an attractive 5'1" brunette with brown eyes, was 30 years old. My father, tall and blond, was almost a year older.

It was already a stormy marriage. Alcohol had consumed my father and taken most of their earthly possessions. Before his death when I was three years old, he had long since abandoned us and was living with another woman. Life was difficult for my mom, both before and after he died. Now at 33 she was a widow, responsible for raising and providing for three children at the close of the Great Depression. But she was incredibly resourceful and wise beyond her years.

I was blissfully unaware that we were "poor." For me, it was simply our way of life. I could not remember any other. Sheltered in the security of my mother's love and that of my older sister Dolores and my older brother Tom, life was good. Several members of our family lived in the same neighborhood, my cousin Alice across the street and my cousin Jerry a stone's throw away. Alice, Jerry and I were all the same age. Jerry had two older sisters, Frances and June.

Dolores was a wonderful big sister to me. I was shy, timid and sensitive, but her temperament matched her beautiful copper red hair. She would defend me like a mother bear her cub, if I needed her to stand up for me. When Dolores was older and employed, she bought my first wristwatch, and I was thrilled with it. How heartbroken I was when I fell on the playground and broke it, not only because it no longer worked but because I had broken something she had given me.

Blond-haired Tom, the oldest at almost thirteen, stepped in where he could to fill the void that was left by our father. As a young boy, he found employment in various places – from a radio repair shop (he was born with a natural talent in electronics) to working in a drug store, and also availing himself of other opportunities to earn an honest dollar. I remember very vividly the Christmas he bought a doll for me, when "Santa" might not have brought much otherwise. He also thought it was his job to help keep me in line when I misbehaved!

What we did not have in material possessions was far surpassed by our wealth in things too valuable for price tags. Our mother maintained her integrity and lovingly cared for each of us in spite of her difficulties. She taught us honesty. We understood that it would be better to go hungry than to lie or steal. She shared with us her love for reading, and our regular trips to the library were enjoyable and important. Books opened up a whole world of dreams and possibilities.

Our home was a little four-room frame house that we rented. We in turn rented out one of the rooms which had its own outside entrance. In our "living room," which also served as a bedroom, my mom, Dolores and I slept together in one double bed – along with Patches, our brindle and white cat. There was no sofa. But there was a rocking chair, a treadle sewing machine which also served as a decorative table when covered with a scarf, and a gas heater. Tom slept on a single bed in the dining room. The remaining room was a kitchen. The bathroom, on the other side of a screened-in back porch, was shared with the renters.

We did not have hot water unless we heated it on the stove, but we did have running water. Our "washing machine" was the bath tub, which my mom activated with a rub board. Her sense of humor came through in a little poem that she wrote out neatly and hung on the bathroom wall:

> *Roses are red,*
> *Violets are blue,*
> *Please flush the toilet*
> *When you get through!*

Natural gas supplied both heat and light; we had no electricity. The gas light mantles were extremely fragile, and at an early age I learned that I must be very careful with them. Beneath one of those gas lights I snuggled in bed to read library books with my mother at night. She taught me to read before I entered school.

Each day's main meal consisted primarily of beans, and here again she exercised creativity, varying the kind of beans we had from day to day – great northerns, pintos, butter beans and so forth. Sometimes she managed to add something extra, like a little meat, to the meal. She remodeled hand-me-down clothes so that they fit nicely. Adding an additional touch of embroidery on a collar made a dress appear more original and less like someone's cast-off.

Having been born with a romantic nature that loved beauty and a mother who liked to keep things looking clean and cheerful, the only thing I remember longing for was a pair of pretty shoes. Our shoes had to be serviceable for all occasions, and so I wore brown oxfords. I dreamed of wearing dainty feminine slippers, but of course did not mention it, understanding that we did not have money for such things. I recall that on one occasion my mother pawned her watch to buy even the serviceable brown oxfords.

One thing I missed, apart from dress shoes, was having a daddy. According to my mom, once I asked, "*Can't we buy us a daddy?*" Well, we found none for sale, and even if we had there was no money to buy one!

But God was about to give a little girl an incredible journey through life, including what she wanted most – a daddy.

CHANGE

Chapter 3

With the exception of my sister Dolores, we did not attend church. As a little girl, Dolores would slip out of bed on Sunday mornings and go to Sunday school at a little Baptist church within walking distance of our house. She liked the little story cards with colored pictures that were given to each child.

Apart from that, our family's attendance at religious meetings was – in my mind – like attending a side show. We went for entertainment, not for religious reasons. At least the adults did. As for me, I would have been happier not to go at all, as the noise and unusual activity — people sometimes even rolling on the floor during the service — were frightening to me. Such meetings were not conducted by the little church Dolores attended but by others, usually in a tent on a vacant lot.

When I was three years old, the small Baptist church in our neighborhood also announced some special services, and my mom and a friend decided to go. These meetings, however, turned out to be warm and friendly services, not the kind that frightened me!

It was there that she heard the gospel, <u>really</u> heard the gospel for the first time. Perhaps she had heard the words before, but that night the ears of her heart were open and sensitive to God's Word and to His voice. She told her friend that when they gave another invitation she was going to go forward. True to her word, on the second night of attendance when an invitation was given she walked forward and publicly declared to the world her faith and trust in the Lord Jesus Christ as her personal Savior.

A few days later, she was baptized, and her thoughts turned to my father. She recalled a past conversation with him when she had said in jest that she thought she'd go down to the Baptist church and get baptized. He laughingly responded, *"You do that, and I'll come and throw rotten eggs at you."* But now, she was being baptized and it was with a sincere desire to proclaim her trust in Jesus Christ as her Savior and to obey His command. As for my father, his body was lying in the morgue after drowning while intoxicated. The woman with whom he had been living came to tell us that he was dead. Now, at the age of thirty-five, my father's life was over. My mother's was beginning anew.

For all of us, life took on a new dimension. Though she had always been a good and loving mother, now her heavy load was lightened by her newfound faith. She began learning hymns and singing them while she worked around the house. As she learned of anything in our life style that she felt needed to be changed, it was changed. Her decision was real and her commitment was total.

We began to attend church regularly, and she became actively involved. The pastor said of her that she was there "every time the doors were open!" Even some of our fun times involved scripture. I remember sitting on the front steps of our house taking turns saying Bible verses we had memorized. Whoever couldn't come up with a verse was "out." The person who could keep going the longest was the winner.

Several years passed and then came the catalyst for the next big change in our lives! Some special meetings were being held in a church across town and a man by the name of Walter Easton, a member of our church, asked my mother if we would like a ride. The church was too far away for us to walk and we had no car. She assumed that he was getting together a group of people to go in his car and accepted the invitation. Imagine her surprise when he arrived at our house alone! That was the beginning, and for the next couple of years I think I went with them on every date.

I loved having him around. One night in exuberant childhood innocence, I invited him to spend the night with us! It seemed logical to me, since I knew he would be coming back again the next day. But he graciously declined my invitation.

My mother had been a widow for seven years when they married. I was ten years old and no one could have been happier about the marriage than I! He became my father and when I talk about "my dad" I am usually referring to him. The two of us played table games together — checkers, dominoes and others. My sister Dolores had moved away from home and my brother Tom was in the United States Navy. I remember one night when the two of us were playing a game and my mother was fixing hot chocolate for us. As I sat there I thought, *"I don't ever want to grow up!"* One day I exclaimed, *"I'm so glad we married him!"* As long as he lived, until the age of 95, we always laughed about when *"we"* married him! Although he was 18 years older than my mother, they had more than 36 years together before he died in 1981.

DARKNESS

Chapter 4

A flickering campfire dispelled some of the darkness of the summer night, as it cast its shadow-
mixed brightness on the young faces seated around it.
A youthful speaker standing in the center of the group
was calling for surrender to Christ. In at least one
fifteen-year-old heart a fierce struggle raged. An invitation was given, and the feet of that fifteen-year-old
almost got out from under her and went forward.
Almost, but not quite. That heart was mine.

The incredibly strong force which seemed to
compel me forward that evening was somehow
resisted. Perhaps it was due to a strong sense of self
preservation – a fear of relinquishing personal plans,
desires, myself.

I can't recall that I ever really liked going to
Sunday school and church as a child, or to Vacation
Bible School in the summer. I went without
complaining or telling my parents how I really felt. I
loved my mom so much that I couldn't stand the

thought of disappointing or hurting her. In fact, I'm not sure that I even admitted my true feelings to myself at that stage of life. How could I be so blasphemous as to say that I didn't enjoy Sunday school and that listening to a choir open the service with the same call to worship every Sunday morning was so monotonous I could hardly bear to sit through it? How could I tell anyone that Christian music, particularly when heard outside the confines of a church, such as over a radio, was depressing to me? I probably would have thought myself very wicked had I confided these feelings even to myself. My heart was full of everything from boredom to fear of what would happen to me if I should suddenly drop dead!

There was a time when I was around seven years old that I did experience an earnest desire to do whatever it took to make myself right with God. As a result, one evening I walked forward to the church altar during an invitation at the close of a worship service. Several other people responded to the invitation that evening and perhaps it was because of this that there was a lack of counseling help available. All I remember is that I was told to "*say yes*" and I could not understand for the life of me how saying "*yes*" would make everything right. Yes to what? But even at that early age my pride finally got the better of me. Without pressing for any further help or clarification and to avoid appearing totally dumb, I said "*yes*" and shortly thereafter was baptized into the membership of the church.

However, as a teenager I began to wonder more and more about the reality of my relationship with

Jesus Christ. By this time I knew – at least in my head – how to become a Christian. In my heart there was a gnawing fear that I was not one.

Dread of being sent to a foreign country and living in primitive conditions among smelly people of a race different from my own pulled at me, magnifying and perpetuating the struggle. Somehow I had the feeling that if I truly committed myself to the Lord Jesus Christ, perhaps this was exactly what He would require. I had my own plans and they didn't include anything like that! My desires seemed reasonable enough: I wanted to become a nurse, have a *"happy ever after"* marriage, live in the proverbial rose-covered cottage and raise a family. I didn't want to exchange these things for God's plan – whatever that plan might be.

That summer night I walked away from the campfire with the empty victory of having succeeded in refusing to respond to the still, soft voice. My will had won out, but something inside me had changed. It felt as if what had been a warm beating heart inside me had become a lump of cold stone. I was numb and empty inside. I had entered the life of inner torment, frustration and fear that is known only by those who willfully reject God.

For almost three years I walked in that darkness, in an inner hell of my own making. I had pushed God away and He had given me my freedom.

Outwardly, things appeared the same. I continued in high school, giving only occasional application to my studies. But God in His grace saw to it that I managed to graduate. This was the goodness of a loving God Who, even though rejected, continued to work out His plans of love for my life. He knew I would need a high school diploma for the steps He had in mind.

Apparently my facade was quite convincing. Neither my family nor my close friends realized that I was not on the inside what my words and actions led them to believe. Church? I was a member and I was there for everything. I yearned to be real, but that yearning was not strong enough to make me willing to give up the mastery of my own desires and plans.

Somewhere along the way I heard a preacher challenging young people by saying that God was looking for young people with courage. Bitterly I thought, *"Well, that lets me out! I'm a coward!"* Later in life, one of my great joys was in learning that what that preacher had said is not true. The Bible says that God is looking for those through whom He can infuse *His* strength and *His* life. 1 Corinthians 1:26-29 says,

> *"But God hath chosen the foolish things of the world to confound the wise; and God hath chosen the weak things of the world to confound the things which are mighty; and base things of the world, and things which are despised, hath God chosen, yea, and things which are not, to bring to nought things that are: That no flesh should glory in his presence."*

A few years later I was filled with joy and encouragement when I read in 2 Chronicles 16:9,

"For the eyes of the Lord run to and fro throughout the whole earth, to shew himself strong in the behalf of them whose heart is perfect toward him . . ."

It is *His* strength and *His* courage that are to be manifested, and He often chooses the most unlikely vessels through which to do it. If He was looking for an unlikely vessel, I certainly qualified on that score! But I did not yet know that truth.

Neither did I know what a precious journey through life He was planning for me.

LIGHT

Chapter 5

Light rejected brings further darkness. My darkness became deeper. My inner misery increased. Life did not seem worth living. I wondered whether it was worth the effort to continue the struggle.

A day came when I locked myself in the bathroom, took off the lid from a bottle of poison and stood looking at its contents. Then I recapped the bottle. In my heart I knew that I was no more prepared to die than I was to live. I was not ready to meet God. I walked out to continue in my misery.

A youth group visited our church to present a program of singing and giving testimonies about the Lord and their love for Him. *"Are they genuine, or are they hypocrites like I am?"* I wondered.

How grateful I am to God for His mercy, love and grace. He continued to work in my life, to patiently wait for my stubborn will to yield to Him, and to wait for my icy cold heart to respond to the warmth of His love.

The darkness in my soul produced doubt and

confusion in my mind. What did it really mean to believe? How <u>could</u> I believe? What did it mean to have the kind of belief that resulted in the salvation of one's soul? How did one get hold of <u>real</u> faith? The Bible says that even the demons believe in God. They recognize Jesus Christ for Who He is.

What was the kind of belief of which the Apostle John wrote in John 1:12,

> *"But as many as received him, to them*
> *gave he power to become the sons of God,*
> *even to them that believe on his name."*

I now wanted to know.

Embarrassed to talk about it with anyone who knew me, my first overt act of seeking help was an anonymous letter to a local radio preacher. As best I could, I poured out my questions. Shortly thereafter, the radio preacher talked about my letter over the air, *"I have an anonymous letter from an eighteen-year-old girl . . ."* As my letter became the center of his message, I felt that I became the target of his condemnation. It had not been my intention to criticize anyone's faith or contend that it was not real. Rather, I desperately wanted to know how it was possible to experience it for myself. I could not produce belief by my own will power and I would not tell myself that I believed something that – no matter how much I wanted to – I did not truly believe.

I do not know exactly what agent God used in bringing me to the place of crisis. But suddenly there I was! It seemed that He was giving me one last chance. I had a strange feeling that if I didn't respond, He would let me go altogether, perhaps ending my physical life.

We were having evangelistic meetings at church, but though my heart was deeply burdened, I still could not bring myself to go to the altar or to ask for help. On the way home after one of the services, however, I knew that I had to share this heavy burden with my mother and stepfather. On hearing my words, they seemed shocked and wanted to assure me that I was a Christian. I could not be so easily persuaded. I asked them to pray with me about it and so before going to bed that night we prayed together.

The following morning I went to the church and talked with the pastor. He did not seem convinced of my need either. Noticing that he looked at his wristwatch while we were talking, I felt he was in a hurry to get on to something he considered more important. Perhaps I seemed only a confused teenager. He tried to assure me with some Scripture verses.

I left the pastor's office still heavy hearted and searching. Then, standing alone in a hallway of the church, I turned to God Himself. *"Oh, God,"* I prayed. *"If I've never been saved, I want to be."* He was there in that empty hallway with me. He understood. He cared. Romans 10:13 says, *"Whosoever shall call on the name of the Lord shall be saved."* It was true!

A short time later during an invitation at the end of a church service, I stepped out of the choir and went to the altar to make a public declaration of my faith in Christ and to request baptism. I don't think I had ever heard of anyone who was already a church member doing such a thing! But it didn't matter. I had reached the end of myself, and when I did He was there! I John 4:10 has been my testimony ever since, *"Herein is love, not that we loved God, but that He loved us."*

I did not experience a great emotional upheaval. It was simply an unlimited surrender after a long battle. I had given myself to Him and received Him as my Savior. It was a total commitment – forever!

As time went by, however, I noticed some dramatic changes! It was as if I had stepped from great darkness into a path filled with sunshine! The sky seemed more blue and the leaves on the trees more beautifully green than I had ever seen them before. I was in touch with the One who had created them and as I reveled in the beauty of His creation my heart was flooded with the joy of His presence. Peace filled my being. The light of a new day, of a new life, had dawned!

My life's journey was on course now.

FAITH

Chapter 6

It was April, I was 18 and spring was beautiful! Life had a glorious new dimension.

However, not everyone understood my joy, this passion for God that He had put within my heart. I was to learn that problems as well as joys come with such a commitment. Satan does not give up easily.

In fact, my new journey with God seemed at times to bring problems of its own and sometimes it brought conflicts as well. Criticism was painful, misunderstandings caused heartache and not knowing how to respond in some situations produced anxiety. In addition, like some of the New Testament Christians, I found myself bound for a while with things which I felt I must do in order to please God. But by His grace, the Lord in time helped me understand more of the liberty that we have in Him. He helped me learn to walk in the leading of the Holy Spirit, remembering that not every "spirit" is of God. I was to learn the wonderful truth that even in the difficult times He is with us!

Since graduation from high school the previous year, I had helped in my parents' neighborhood grocery store. But I began to sense that God was leading me to do something else, and in November a position as receptionist/secretary for a physician in the area became available. It was my first real job. The Bible says that we are to perform our duties well and as unto God Himself, not just for a human employer, so I tried hard to be a very good worker. That was my job, but He was my life.

Hymns no longer depressed me, as they had earlier. In fact, their words expressed many of my own personal feelings. As I sang or listened to them, they became a part of my communication with this wonderful God, my Father. Within me sprang an insatiable desire to study the Word of God, to spend time alone with Him. Being with His people became such a joy that I didn't want to stay away from anything that was going on at church any night of the week.

My heart yearned for fellowship with God and I found myself wanting to share this wonderful new life with others. One evening each week I went out with others from our church seeking to do just that. A growing burden for people who had never even had a chance to hear the good news blossomed within my heart. Sharing with people in my own area continued important, but more and more I thought of those who were unreached. Local people had so many churches from which to choose and also Christian radio programs to help them. Some people in the world had nothing.

After working for a while, I saved enough money to buy a car. I did not know how to drive a car, but after buying one my stepfather taught me to drive. I gave the car a name: Betsy! One of the most precious contributions Betsy made to my life was that she enabled me to drive to a wooded area where I could spend time completely alone with the Lord. Sometimes I'd take a girlfriend with me. She had come to know the Lord shortly after I did and seemed to understand my feelings in a way none of the other young people did. Sometimes, particularly on Sunday afternoons, we'd go to the wooded area and listen to Christian radio broadcasts on the car radio, or just talk together, or pray.

Other times I would go alone, sit in the quietness of the woods and read. I read about Christians who had tremendous faith and in whose lives God did wonderful things. It seemed incredible that people who lived long before I was born had experienced the same things that I was experiencing. Maybe when we are young, it seems that everyone who went before us or who is older has always been old and has never experienced the same emotions, doubts and decisions that we do! I was in awe as I lived their journeys through life with them by means of their writings or stories about them.

There was Hudson Taylor, the founder of the China Inland Mission (now Overseas Missionary Fellowship). Hudson Taylor was born in England in 1832, over 100 years before I was born. But in reading about his life, I felt that he could easily have been a contemporary. Here was a man who had complete confidence in God's faithfulness. At the age of seventeen, almost the same as my age, his life had been transformed by Jesus Christ.

Hudson Taylor's life was filled with adventure, but it was not the adventure that attracted me. It was his utmost confidence in God, his seeking to know God's will, and seeing God respond to this that stirred and challenged my own heart. He was not a big man physically, but he had faith in God Who was able to do big things through him. He experienced a normal range of emotions and struggles. There was his romance with his beloved Maria, his great grief at the loss of their firstborn and later the loss of two of his other children and eventually even his dear Maria.

As missionaries in China they suffered illnesses. They knew what it meant to be physically exhausted, to face financial and material needs, to cope with the misunderstandings of other missionaries. But through it all, God sustained them and used them in a way that still impacts the world well over 100 years later. After losing Maria, God brought a second wife, Jenny, into Hudson's life and gave them three children, two by birth and one by adoption.

Then there was George Mueller, another man in England, who did not have a lot of money of his own, but felt God's leading to provide orphanage care for two thousand children. His conviction, like that of Hudson Taylor, was to make his needs known only to God. God not only provided for the orphanage work, sometimes at what seemed the last minute, but also enabled him to send funds to help Hudson Taylor.

As I learned about these people and others like them, I wanted that kind of faith. I wanted to trust God more. I loved God with all my heart and wanted to be and do what He wanted, but I did not know how to acquire that kind of faith. I talked with Him about it. *"Dear God,"* I prayed, *"How can I have more faith?"* In response, He led my attention to a particular verse in the Bible, found in Romans 10:17. *"So then faith cometh by hearing, and hearing by the word of God."*

What a wonderful revelation! He has promised that if we immerse ourselves in His word, He will increase our faith. He was lovingly preparing me for the next steps of the journey.

CLOUDS

Chapter 7

I don't think that I had ever really thought of moving away from my home town, of living anywhere else. I had settled into a job I liked and was deeply involved in the life of my church. But somehow a feeling that changes might lie ahead was developing within me. I began to wonder where I would be in another five years.

A high school teacher had said that I was a dreamer, and she was probably correct. But the exciting days, years and adventures that lay ahead of me could not have been imagined in my wildest dreams. Nevertheless somehow, deep down inside me, I sensed that walking with God was going be a great adventure!

Then what seemed to me a tragedy entered my life. I was not feeling well and was becoming more and more exhausted and losing weight. I was hospitalized for some testing, with the doctor saying that he felt I had either a kidney problem or a liver problem.

A kidney problem sounded so dull and so unfeminine! It seemed that a more dramatic disability would be more acceptable, something that had more flair to the diagnosis! But I had perhaps underestimated kidney problems! They may not sound very glamorous, but they can be very devastating.

The test results did not look good. I was informed that the testing had revealed an enlarged kidney. Its removal was considered and the advice of a specialist was obtained. They decided against removing the kidney at that time, choosing rather to treat me for the poison that had built up in my system. I was told that I would probably need treatments about every six to nine months to clear out the poison that would build up in my system.

I was also advised that I needed at least ten hours of rest each night and that I should give up either my job or my church work. What a crushing blow to my dreams! Was I becoming a semi invalid?

I did not understand what God was doing. Now that I wanted to serve Him, why was this happening? *"Why couldn't it have happened to someone who wasn't going to serve him anyway?,"* I thought! Although I couldn't realistically compare myself with an important person like Joseph in the Bible, I could at least to a degree relate to what he must have felt. He'd had a great dream and then he found himself in a pit!

I continued seeing the specialist and accepting any treatment prescribed. But I simply could not give up my church involvement! Nor could I quit my job.

I began teaching eleven-year-old girls in Sunday school and at first everything I could think of to say about the whole lesson could be covered in fifteen minutes! But, even though I could not teach very well, I tried to let the girls know that I cared about them and faithfully explained how they could know the Lord. I had parties for them, at which I always gave a devotional message. As another class activity, we visited shut-ins. Then in addition to the Sunday school class, I began working with a group of younger children at the church on Wednesday afternoons, my afternoon off from the office.

With all my heart I wanted to serve the Lord well, but felt terribly inadequate. Then I learned of an organization called the Child Evangelism Fellowship. CEF is an interdenominational and international ministry to children. It reaches out through neighborhood classes and backyard Bible clubs to present the plan of salvation and teach the Bible to children. They also train volunteers how to do this. Gladys and Albert Hess, a young couple who had been in charge of our youth group in a previous church, had become involved with this ministry and were now the City Directors of the Child Evangelism Fellowship in Fort Smith. I asked Gladys if she would be willing to help me with one of my classes. She agreed and was a tremendous asset.

Gladys took me under her wing. We'd meet in her home and study topics like prayer, victorious Christian living, and so forth from the CEF teacher training manuals. She also invited me to attend a CEF teacher training class and prayer meeting with her. I loved it! Fellowship with the people involved in that work was a wonderful source of inspiration and spiritual encouragement to me.

However, more clouds loomed on the horizon. Our church was very denominationally oriented and not open to interdenominational ministries. My pastor did not support my relationship with the Child Evangelism Fellowship. A couple of times I was called into his office and exhorted about my mistake in becoming involved with CEF. On one occasion the pastor said, *"Helen, you can't attend those prayer meetings and be loyal to your church."* The simple response that sprang from my heart declared, *"My loyalty is to the <u>Lord</u>."* On another occasion the pastor preached against the organization from the pulpit. To my knowledge, I was the person present who was involved with CEF.

If the pastor did not understand, how could I blame my parents for not understanding? I was young and inexperienced. But God's leading seemed so real, and I could not deny the oneness and fellowship in the Lord that I felt with the CEF workers. How does one prove something is right when it is known only in the heart?

Through the city directors of CEF, I became acquainted with the State CEF Directors for Arkansas, Bernard and Margaretha Wiebe. They were a wonderful couple and great encouragers. The need for a secretary in the state CEF office in the capital city of Little Rock was shared with me. After serious consideration and an overnight visit with the Wiebes in their home in Little Rock, I accepted the position and resigned my job in the doctor's office.

But before I could move from Fort Smith to Little Rock, my parents opposed my decision so strongly that the Wiebes advised me to cancel my plans. Mr. Wiebe phoned me at the office to let me know that my stepfather had phoned them long distance. Long distance calls were not as routinely made at that time in our lives as they are today, and so it was an especially meaningful action on my stepfather's part.

I was legally old enough to have insisted on going. But neither the Wiebes nor I felt that it was the right thing to do at that point. We knew that my parents simply didn't understand. They were acting out of love for me, wanting to protect me from what they felt was a wrong decision. Not being familiar with interdenominational work or with the Child Evangelism Fellowship, as far as they knew I could have been involving myself with some kind of cult. The Wiebes told me that, for my parents sake, they would send a letter to my home address verifying the change in plans.

Now what? I was stunned. I had resigned my job and someone else had been hired to take my place! However, when the doctors learned that my plans had fallen through, they offered to keep me on the office staff. One of them said graciously, *"We realize now that you have been doing the work of two people, so we'll just keep both of you!"*

Though not able to move to Little Rock and enter a ministry with CEF or to have the help of the CEF Director in my class at church any longer, my

friendship with the Hesses and the Wiebes continued. Our points of contact were my office and the
Hesses' home.

It looked like a dead end, but in reality my journey was getting underway!

DECISION

Chapter 8

I have learned that God has many ways and awe inspiring methods of providing guidance. One Saturday evening, the sensation of a crushing burden, a feeling of heaviness, descended on my heart as I went to bed. I didn't know what was wrong. Getting out of bed and kneeling beside it, I prayed, "*Lord, if You're trying to show me something, I want to do Your will.*" Crawling back into bed and snuggling under the sheet, I promptly fell asleep.

As Sunday morning dawned, however, I awoke to find that the same heavy-burdened feeling had returned. Not understanding it and knowing nothing further to do, I prepared to leave for Sunday school and church with my parents as usual.

When we arrived at the church, there was a message for me. Someone had called the church office and left a request for me to return the call. The message was from my friend Gladys, the City Director for the local CEF work, who asked if I could come over to her house later that day. I was happy to do that and after lunch that Sunday afternoon I got into Betsy and drove to her home. Gladys shared that she had felt burdened to discuss with me the possibility of my attending the International Child Evangelism Institute in Muskegon, Michigan.

Leaving her home and climbing back into Betsy, I headed for my wooded sanctuary. There, alone with the Lord in the beauty of the woods, I poured out my heart to Him and waited quietly before Him. *"Lord, if this is what You are trying to show me, I'm willing to go to this school."* I had never been to Michigan, but if God wanted me to go it didn't matter whether the school was in Michigan or Timbuktu! I really gave no thought to how far it was or what was involved in getting there. If God was taking me, it would be all right. The burdened feeling that I had sensed since the previous night rolled away and was replaced with a flood of peace! The decision was made. I would resign my job — again. I would step out by faith. I would go.

The first big hurdle and the one I dreaded most was that of telling my parents. Not only was I about to go hundreds of miles away, but I was going to enroll in a school operated by the International Child Evangelism Fellowship! However, they must be told. God would help me. He encouraged me greatly and confirmed His leading through a Bible verse in Joshua 1:9,

> *"Have not I commanded thee?" Be strong and of a good courage; be not afraid, neither be thou dismayed: for the Lord thy God is with thee whithersoever thou goest."*

The third word in that verse, the pronoun *"I,"* stood out as if illuminated! It would be painful to go against the wishes of those I loved most, but God was clearly leading. That verse would sustain me through many difficult experiences and joys in the years ahead.

On the evening I had chosen as the night to tell my parents, I sat alone in my room waiting for them to come home and looking to the Lord for grace and strength to face the moment of crisis. The moment came and it was no easier than I had anticipated. Something like a cloud came over my stepfather's face when I told them of my decision. It cut through me like a knife and it broke my heart to hurt them. I loved them so much. But I also loved the Lord and knew that His will was the deciding factor. God's will would be best for all of us.

Again I resigned my job at the doctor's office, advising them that I would be leaving at the end of May to attend school in Michigan. Things seemed on course. I was hardly prepared for the next blow!

That blow came in the form of a letter from the International Child Evangelism Institute, which reached me at the office. Because of the opposition at home, my communication with CEF now came through the office where I worked. The letter told me that my application to the CEF Institute had been rejected!

Apparently the International Child Evangelism Institute was designed for training people who already had some Bible institute or college background. I had never even heard of a Bible institute!

Knowing how poorly I had applied myself throughout high school, I was already somewhat apprehensive about going to the Institute, but since it seemed that this was God's plan I was confident that He would help me. However, now ICEI had suggested that I attend a Bible school and then reapply for their course of study. I held the letter in my hands in disbelief, stunned and confused. It had seemed that God was leading so clearly. I decided not to say anything to anyone about it as yet.

But God was not shaken; He was still in charge. In His gracious providence and perfect timing, Bernard Wiebe, CEF director for the state of Arkansas, came to town a little later that very same day and stopped by the office for a brief visit with me. I didn't tell him about the letter, but decided to wait until the shock had subsided a little and we could have an opportunity to talk privately.

That evening, at the home of the home of Gladys and Albert Hess where Mr. Wiebe was staying during his visit to the Fort Smith area, I shared this latest news with all of them. It was a blow to them as well. They had been in full agreement and totally supportive of the step I was taking. We had all felt that it was of God.

We discussed the situation and our concern over it. Then Mr. Wiebe went into another room and made a long distance call from Arkansas to California, where the CEF headquarters office was located at that time. I did not hear the conversation, but in a little while he came to us with incredible news. *"You've just been accepted!"* he declared with a big smile.

How wonderful the Lord is, and how gracious! I did not share this temporary upheaval with my family or with my employers. As far as they knew, it was set that I was going from the time I made the announcement.

God was leading and my journey was continuing step by step.

MICHIGAN

Chapter 9

Travel arrangements and finances were the next items on the agenda. I did not have much money, but the Bible says that when God puts forth His sheep He goes before them and that He cares for them. Selling my well-used car would not provide a fortune, or even enough money for the entire summer, but it would get me started. God could be trusted for the remainder and for the future beyond that. So I sold my car and bought two inexpensive suitcases and a one-way bus ticket to Muskegon, Michigan.

It was the first time I had ever gone so far from home alone – almost 900 miles. My first big journey involved going where I had never been, spending the summer with people I had never met, and traveling hundreds of miles alone by bus. But my natural bent toward timidity was overcome by the confidence that I was in God's will.

When the day came for my departure, my parents were willing to take me to the bus depot in

Fort Smith. Heartache was a heavy weight for all three of us as we said our goodbyes, and I boarded the bus and headed north.

Settling back into the bus seat, looking out the window, and going alone into an unknown future, momentarily I was tempted to look back — back to the safety of my room with the ruffled curtains at the windows, the comfort of having my parents and family nearby and the familiarity and security of a good job. Then I reminded myself that — even if just for a moment – there was a temptation to look back, that would be like the Israelites longing for the leeks and garlic after being freed from their captivity and led out of Egypt. It seemed a little scary, but at the same time there was the sense of relaxation that came with being past the crises of the previous months. I knew that I did not really want to look back or to turn back. The sense of freedom and excitement about the future was dampened only by the heartache I was causing my parents. I hoped that in time that they would understand, and I was determined to do everything within my power to keep reminding them that I loved them.

I was not really alone. God was with me, just as He promised. After many hours on the road, the big bus pulled into the city of Chicago. I had never been in such a big city, a beautiful city with tall stately buildings and the largest bus terminal that I had ever seen.

Then to my dismay, after reaching Chicago I learned that the Continental Trailways bus on which I was traveling did not go to Muskegon, Michigan! It was true that the ticket I had purchased was sufficient to get me to Muskegon, but I must transfer to a Greyhound Bus for the last lap of the journey. That would not have been so much of a problem if they had used the same bus depot. But they didn't and I had no idea how to find the Greyhound Bus Station. So there I stood, a young woman from a small town, in the big city of Chicago for the first time, with two heavy suitcases, very little money, and the need to get myself and the suitcases from one bus station to another. The Greyhound station turned out to be about two city blocks away.

From where he came or where he went, I do not know. But what I do recall is that suddenly a young man dressed in a United States army uniform approached me. I do not know how he knew my plight. Perhaps he had overheard my discussion at the ticket counter. He spoke to me, offered to show me the way and said he would help me get my luggage to the Greyhound station. True to his word, he walked with me down the big city street from station to station carrying my two suitcases. Perhaps he was an angel wearing a soldier's uniform. At least he was that as far as I was concerned!

Relieved and settled aboard the Greyhound bus as it pulled out of Chicago on the last lap of my journey from Arkansas to Muskegon, Michigan, I looked around at the other passengers. A few rows away sat a young woman about my age with a Bible on her lap. What an encouraging note. I made her acquaintance and learned that she, too, was on her way to the International Child Evangelism Institute.

I had looked forward to meeting other people who shared my convictions and now that was happening.

Being a novice at travel, I don't think that I had notified the school of my intended arrival time, nor had I had not known how I would get to the school at Wolfe Lake after getting to Muskegon. But someone was meeting the other young woman and would transport me as well. One other student joined us at the Muskegon bus station and the three of us happily made our way together to the Wolfe Lake campus.

It was a thrilling summer, filled with making new friends and drinking in scriptural, doctrinal and practical living classes, along with learning how to prepare teaching materials. In addition to our studies, time was also allowed for us to swim in the lake and enjoy other activities throughout the week. On Sundays my roommate Louise Moore – a Bible institute graduate who was headed for missionary service in Africa — and I, along with a couple of other students shared in the services of an African-American church in the area. God had laid a special love for that race on my heart. Having come from the segregated south of the 1950's, it was a joy to experience the freedom of participating in the Lord's work with them.

Then the summer was ending, the days in Michigan were drawing to a close, and it was time to settle my account with the school. I was out of money and still owed $40, but when I went to the school office to discuss it, I was told that someone had paid $20 for me. The school was willing to wait for the balance of $20 still due.

What was the next step in God's plan for me? To begin with, I had no funds to finance a return trip to Arkansas. The funds from the sale of my car had been depleted by the travel to Michigan and by the summer's expenses. But school was closing and I must move on. If I returned home to Arkansas, what would I do there? I was told of a couple of areas in other parts of the United States where full time Child Evangelism workers were needed. Perhaps one of these opportunities would be a possibility for me.

Or, what about pursuing further studies? During the summer I had learned about Bible institutes, schools where one can go for an education and for biblical studies in particular. In a counseling session with the missions director at ICEI, he advised me to consider enrolling in one. *"If God leads you to go overseas you will be required to have that training,"* he said. *"And if you feel led to stay in this country you will be better equipped to serve in your local church."* Since I was from the south, two schools there were recommended. I thought and prayed and then decided that Mid-South Bible Institute, a small school in Memphis, Tennessee, was where I should go.

I applied to the school and was accepted. Somehow God would get me there. Where God guides, He provides. Sometimes His supply arrives in what seems to us just in the nick of time, but His timing is right. He gives us opportunities to believe that, to trust Him and to mature in our relationship with Him.

My plans were made. Now it was just a matter of awaiting God's provision.

TENNESSEE

Chapter 10

S ometimes God's provision comes in unexpected ways. A letter came from my mother, unexpectedly telling me that my stepfather wanted to pay for my transportation back to Arkansas when school closed in Michigan. Even though I had told them that I was planning to go to Memphis, TN, after a short time at home, he was willing to see that I got back to Arkansas. God had provided and when the course of studies in Michigan was completed I returned home.

Soon after arriving back in Fort Smith, I went over to visit my friend Gladys and her family and was encouraged to learn that she and her husband wanted to pay the remaining $20 that I owed to the International Child Evangelism Institute. I was free to go to Tennessee and enroll in the Bible institute! As yet I had no money for travel to Memphis or for school, but I was free of debt and ready to go when God opened the door.

As with attending ICEI, my parents did not approve of my attending the school in Memphis. It was painful to have this conflict between us, but again I realized that it was their love that tried to discourage me. My stepfather offered to pay my tuition if I would go to a denominational school in Arkansas as an alternative to enrolling in the Bible institute in Tennessee. It was his way of seeking to find a compromise between my desire to study in a Christian school and their desire to keep me in the state and away from an interdenominational school. His kindness was appreciated, but my heart contended, *"No, I'd rather go where God wants me and let Him pay the way."*

The God who had led me to Michigan, gotten me through the summer and provided for my return to Arkansas would take me the rest of the way.

As it turned out, my parents were going to Florida for a vacation that fall, and they told me that since they would be driving through Memphis anyway, they would arrange it at the time I needed to go and would take me to the school. If I changed my mind about staying there, I could simply continue on the vacation trip with them.

Shortly before we left Fort Smith to begin our journey, my mother found me alone in the kitchen and handed me $50 in cash, *"just in case"* this really was God's will for me. They were not wealthy, but a mother's love did not want me stranded without funds. Perhaps, too, she was beginning to sense that I really was following God's leading.

We arrived in Memphis — my parents, my heavy

heart and I — and located the school on Poplar Avenue. We pulled into the driveway and they waited outside for me to go in and check out things. Perhaps somehow it would not work out and I would go on to Florida with them, returning our lives to normal.

On entering the school lobby, I found the administrative office near the front entrance. With the strong conviction that this was exactly where God wanted me, I didn't discuss my financial shortage or any other problem. There would be plenty of time for that later. I had been accepted as a student and so simply informed them that I was there!

My things were unloaded from the car and my parents and I said our goodbyes. They continued their journey and I continued mine. It would be a few months before we would see each other again. My heart ached that there was discord between us. There was no hostility on either side, just heartache. We both felt we were doing the right thing.

My luggage was carried to the second floor and into the girls dormitory, where I was ushered into my room. It was a cheerful room with two twin beds, two desks and a window to the outside. Another crisis was past and I had entered another safe haven. This would be my home, my life, for a while. I would be blessed with new friends among people who shared my beliefs.

It was there that I met a young woman who was not only my new roommate but who was destined to become one of my closest friends. Lorene McIntyre and I became as close as sisters and she has remained a loyal friend to this day. An attractive 5'2" blond, she looked at her tall 5'8" roommate, noticed that my eyes were red and wondered if I had been crying. She didn't ask. She just welcomed me and let me know that she was glad we would be roommates.

Lorene had also come through a difficult situation. Her family had not been in favor of her coming to Mid-South either. As with me, she had little or no money. Lorene was a few years younger than I at 18. I was 22, almost 23. Our backgrounds were different; she had grown up on a farm and I had grown up in the city. But our hearts had the same goal, the same deep love for the Lord and the same desire to do His will. That is what has bound us together over the years.

Two young women with virtually no money, but who felt that God was leading and that He could be trusted to provide, had found themselves together in a dorm room in Memphis. Once again I was settling into a new city, a new school and among people who loved the Lord and wanted to know the Bible. Ground was being laid for the continuing journey on which God was leading me.

Lorene obtained a part-time job in the school kitchen and dining room, and since I had over three years of office experience a part-time secretarial job at the school was made available to me. I worked in the office for four hours every day after school and a half day on Saturdays. We were both grateful for God's provision for our needs. In spite of the dire predictions about my health a year earlier, I was leading a pretty normal life.

We had a wonderful housemother, Mom Johnson,

who quickly became a surrogate mother to all of us. She had a ready smile, a caring spirit and a deep love for the Lord.

We reveled in our studies. As we studied the scriptures it was as if a spiritual banquet had been set before our hungry souls and we drank in the sound biblical teaching. I had not been really interested in studying during high school days, but now I had a thirst to learn. I not only enjoyed the wonderful Bible studies, but also other subjects such as English, Greek, psychology, logic, public speaking and a variety of other courses. The school was small, but the faculty was top notch! The smallness of the school enabled us to be like a family, praying for one another and caring for one another's needs.

Somehow, even though Lorene and I both carried a full load of studies and worked to support ourselves, we managed to have our fun times. We made a great team for getting into trouble! One thing we discovered was that there are multiple uses for an ironing board! It is amazing how easily an ironing board with a scarf on its head can be mistaken for a person. We dressed it up and sat it on a commode in a bathroom stall in the dormitory. When someone opened the door to the stall, a quick glance made them think that they had opened the door on another person! Naturally they closed the door too quickly to realize that there was no one there! Sometimes the act even evoked an apology to the empty stall – empty, that is, except for an ironing board with a scarf on its head!

One night we decided to put the ironing board into the bed of a classmate who had stayed out after hours. Her room was next to Mom Johnson's, and when she returned she quietly prepared to slip into bed in the dark. There was a blood curdling scream that brought the housemother running as the student uncovered a "stranger" in her bed!

During one exam week, the ironing board committed suicide on the floor in the hallway outside the dining room. Complete with ketchup for blood she presented quite a spectacle at first glance.

During a chapel message one morning, Dr. James Crichton, the college president, declared that Christians should arise each morning with a song in their hearts. Lorene and I decided to help. Early the next morning, about 5:30, we stood in the small living room surrounded by dorm bedrooms and loudly sang *"Heavenly Sunshine!"* It didn't seem that the Christians in the girls dorm awoke with either sunshine or with a song in their hearts that day. It was more like they awoke ready to throw a shoe at us!

After a while, whenever anything went wrong the first cry out of Mom Johnson's mouth was *"Helen, Lorene!"* One day she exclaimed, *"Helen, when you first came you were so quiet that I thought you were in your room brushing your wings. Now I know that you were in there polishing your horns!"*

During my freshman year it was my privilege to sing with a gospel team and travel with several other students, representing the school in various churches. One Sunday night we were late getting back to the campus, as we had been to Kentucky for a service. On arrival in the dorm, we found that

Lorene and another student had placed a sign on the bathroom door advising us that the commodes were out of order. Some tin cans had been placed in the bathroom with a note that said, *"Use these instead."* The next day we learned that there had been nothing wrong with the plumbing. The next night Lorene and at least one other student found rocks beneath their sheets when they went to bed!

During my second year I enjoyed the opportunity to serve as associate editor for the school yearbook and then in my third year as editor. In the fourth year I was elected class president. Life was truly full.

All of the students had Christian service assignments outside of the school. For me, this included a variety of activities from teaching Sunday school at Bellevue Baptist Church in Memphis to sharing in jail services, working at the rescue mission and teaching children in a Child Evangelism Class in a housing project in Memphis.

Life is not all fun, games and mountain top experiences. So there were times when we, too, faced discouragement, illnesses, bills as they came due as well as other financial needs (things like postage, personal needs, etc.), and physical weariness. The thrilling part came, though, as we saw God provide over and over – for the mental, physical, emotional, spiritual and financial challenges.

Here is one story of God's loving care in very practical matters, as written in my journal,

> *The Lord has been so wonderful . . . in*
> *His provision. Oh, sure, I've missed a few*

meals or had to walk for lack of busfare or things like that once in a while. But those things have not hurt. Had they really been necessary, He would have taken care of them and given them.

Yesterday morning I was out of soap, had squeezed and squeezed to get a little more toothpaste out of the tube, and had no busfare to get to the Child Evangelism class yesterday afternoon. (It is too far to walk within the hour I have between time off work and time for class to start. Also, the other two girls with whom I work in the class would be expecting me to ride the bus.)

Before lunch someone gave me $2.00 to pay for my donation on the lounge fund which the students are responsible to raise. Thirty cents of that went for busfare. Then I had the opportunity to babysit last night. So I went to the store and bought toothpaste and soap and a package of crackers with peanut butter in them for tonight (no supper served on Sunday nights). The babysitting money replaced what I borrowed from the money to give to the lounge fund. And to top all that off, Mom (housemother) paid me for my work in the kitchen last Thursday night. So I am able to meet another small debt I was hoping to meet by tomorrow.

The Lord also recently sent me a nice dress to wear to church. Mom Johnson said the lady who brought it said she felt compelled to bring it, and if no one could wear it she could still wear it herself.

What a wonderful life this is! It's added freshness and something of wonder to my life to be able to really enjoy a nice new bar of soap and plenty of toothpaste. How wonderful it is to see how God works. "For this God is our God for ever and ever: He will be our guide even unto death."

That is just one story of God's gracious provision. There were many more and also many yet to come.

GUIDANCE

Chapter 11

There was a large, old and beautiful tree on the campus, visible from the window of the stairway landing between the first and second floors of the school. Each autumn as I stood on that landing looking out of that window and observing the changing season, feelings of awe tugged at my heart. Another year at this precious place was falling into the passing seasons of my life. What was to come after these four years were finished? What did God want me to do?

My heart was becoming more and more burdened about foreign missions. But I could not say for sure that I was being called into that work. How did one know? What I did know was that my burden and longing to serve as a missionary did not spring from within myself. A few years earlier that was the last thing I would have wanted to do! Now, it seemed the most wonderful option if I were but called and given the opportunity.

Then came a memorable Thursday morning. It was the last week of April in my junior year. I did not have a first period class that day and was sitting in the living room of our dorm working on a term paper. Looking out the window, as I often do when deep in thought or prayer, a little boy caught my eye. He was passing by on his way to school. My mind wandered from term papers and books to a land where men, women, boys and girls live without the Lord. Suddenly I *knew*. I must begin preparing to serve in such a place!

Because of past health problems, it seemed questionable that I would be accepted by a mission board. But the call was not to worry about that. I must plan to go and if I got there it would be because God ordained it. It had become suddenly so clear and definite. I had long hoped for a day when I might have such assurance of God's leading and of His plan for my life. Now that it was here it was precious in its simplicity, "*a still small voice*."

Leaving the work on my term paper, I arose, went to my room and knelt to pray, committing myself afresh to God. The restlessness and conflicting feelings that I had been experiencing lifted and real peace took their place. In my journal I wrote,

> "*Father, thank You for Proverbs 3:5-6.
> 'Trust in the Lord with all thine heart; and
> lean not upon thine own understanding . In
> all thy ways acknowledge him, and he shall
> direct thy paths.' *"

The school (now called Mid-South Bible College,

having attained college status) had scheduled a spring retreat for early May 1960 in a beautiful wooded area of Mississippi, not far from Memphis. I decided that as soon as we returned to school after the retreat I would mail a letter of inquiry to a foreign mission board and then leave it to God to open or close the door. The administrative staff asked me to teach Sunday school for all the women students at the retreat on Sunday morning, and I chose a topic that was very close to my heart, "*the will of God.*"

The Mississippi woods were beautiful that spring week end. The fresh greenness of the trees and the sparkling waters of the lake were inviting. On Saturday morning I sat alone beside the water for a while, reading my Bible. Little did I know how meaningful those moments and the words I was reading would become. Before the day was over, a simple activity would threaten to change my life forever!

Later in the day, Lorene and I decided to go for a swim. For safety's sake we stayed together and did not venture out into the water alone. As there were poisonous snakes, water moccasins, in one end of the lake, we went to the area considered safer for swimming. A sliding board there tempted our youthful and carefree spirits, and we happily climbed the steps to its top. Down the slide and toward the water I flew. Then suddenly, as I landed in the water, excruciating pain shot from my left foot through my body! I did not know what had happened, but tried to turn around to warn Lorene not to come. However, the pain and shock temporarily rendered me unable to make a sound. Later I learned that my left foot had come down on a broken soft drink bottle with the impact strengthened by the force of having come down the sliding board. Mercifully the foot quickly became numb. The bottle must have rolled out of the way as Lorene did not land on it.

How I got out of the water I am not sure, but I remember that one of the students with medical experience from military service secured clean dish towels and applied pressure to the wound. He and another student rushed me to a nearby rural hospital, wisely elevating my bleeding foot by propping it on the dashboard of the car as we traveled.

A surgeon from Memphis had been helping temporarily at the small hospital and was preparing to leave. But he was still there when we arrived and stayed to check me, then hurried me to operating room. As I lay on a gurney being rolled down the hallway to surgery, I felt that God was speaking to me through a scripture verse I had read that very morning beside the lake. It was Matthew 5:16, *"Let your light so shine before men, that they may see your good works, and glorify your Father which is in heaven."* Was I somehow going to glorify God through this experience? The surgeon was capable, but he could not promise that I would ever walk normally again.

Judging from the injury, he said that the broken soft drink bottle must have been standing upright when I landed on it, and it had rolled over gouging out the bottom of my foot, severing five tendons and destroying one in the process. Was God closing the door to missionary service before I even got started?

When I was discharged from the Mississippi hospital and returned to school in Memphis several days later, the surgeon was back at his post in Memphis. That made my postoperative care more convenient for all of us.

A Mid-South Bible College professor and his wife, Paul and Dorothy Davidson, former missionaries in Brazil, had become dear friends. In fact, I worked with Mr. Davidson in the school office. Mrs. Davidson drove back to Mississippi to visit me in the hospital and brought some school books so that I could study. After I returned to Memphis and was able to be out of bed, they rented a wheel chair for me. It was necessary to keep my foot and leg, now encased in a cast, elevated. The wheelchair enabled me to do that and at the same time kept me mobile enough to return to classes and to my job.

Male students carried me from the first to the second floor of the building and back as needed, as there was no elevator. A girls dorm, dining room, library and two classrooms were on the second floor. Other classrooms, offices, the chapel and the bookstore were on the first floor.

On June 3, 1960, a little over three weeks after the accident, graduation night rolled around. Donning my cap and gown, I sat in the wheel chair as one of the students pushed it down the aisle. The chair squeaked as the wheels turned, breaking the somber quietness of the auditorium. It gave me an almost irrepressible urge to giggle! This was my second graduation from Mid-South, as I had previously graduated from the one-year Bible study program. This time it was graduation from the three-year Bible Institute program, and next year it would be graduation from the four-year college program.

The doctor gave me good news when he said that I might be walking without crutches by July. The college allowed me to keep a full time job during the summer months, working from the wheel chair.

Each summer Lorene and I stayed in Memphis and worked during the summer vacations. The first summer, I went on a trip with my parents immediately after school closed and Lorene found an apartment for us while I was gone. It was a cozy little third-floor apartment, apparently a converted attic, and it was within walking distance of the college. Neither of us had a car.

When I returned from the trip, my parents and I stopped by the college bookstore to pick up a key to the apartment. Lorene was not in the bookstore at the moment, but had left the key for me, along with instructions on how to find the apartment. We found the street, a comfortable looking area with typically southern houses, some of which had been turned into apartment houses. We parked the car, unloaded and lugged all my things up to the third floor and stacked them on the floor near the door. Then I inserted the key into the lock and attempted to open the door — but the key did not work! To my chagrin, we learned that we had unloaded my things in the wrong house!

The second summer, we had a larger apartment on the second-floor of a house, which we shared with classmate Sylvia Tatum.

And now for our third summer, we were blessed with a spacious apartment which we shared with some other students. It was on the ground floor of a house, and that was very helpful since I was still in a cast and using the wheel chair. Lorene and I took a summer school class at the college from 6:00 a.m. to 9:00 a.m. and so the days began early. She faithfully pushed my wheelchair down Poplar Avenue to the college early each morning. After the class sessions, we worked full time at the school for the remainder of the day.

By July, I was allowed to begin putting 50 to 75 per cent of my weight on the injured foot with the use of crutches. Then the surgeon gave permission to walk for a few minutes at night without the crutches.

The future loomed ahead with all its questions. I did not know the way, but I had a great Guide and He was in charge of my journey!

TEAM

Chapter 12

Our senior year began in September 1960 and we moved back into the dorm. I was walking again and even able to wear dress shoes that September for the first time since the accident in May. For the second year in a row, my roommate that year was a beautiful young woman from Park Ridge, Illinois who also became a special friend, Sylvia Hansen. Lorene and I had been assigned to different dorms. Maybe that was the best way to keep us out of trouble!

Three part-time jobs and a full load of studies plus extracurricular activities kept my senior year busy. One role was that of student supervisor of our dorm, which meant being on call twenty-four hours a day as substitute housemother and problem handler. Another job, which took just one night a week, was at Bellevue Baptist Church where I helped direct junior recreation on Wednesday evenings. Monday through Saturday I worked my regular schedule in the college office.

By now it appeared that the injury to my foot would not disqualify me from missionary service. I was able to walk normally, perhaps with just a slight limp when extra tired. The doctor mentioned that he had another patient with a similar injury who would never walk normally again. I was blessed and very grateful for my recovery.

October brought me back to the decision of the previous April. Again I wrote in my journal,

> *"This seems a reasonable decision. Apply to a mission board, trusting God to close the way if this is not His will."*

Apparently the injury to my foot – for whatever reason the accident had occurred – had not been intended to close the door to the possibility of missionary service.

With that settled, other questions followed. To what country was God leading me? And with what mission board? Was there a specific ministry for which I should aim? There were so many different types of missionary work: orphanages, teaching opportunities, medical work and general missionary work, to name a few.

I wrote down all the things I could think of that might produce answers to these questions. They included such facts as a God-given love for the black race, a desire to reach those who have never heard the Gospel and particularly those who did not yet have a written language. As I prayed and gleaned information about different world areas, my interest focused more and more on Dutch New Guinea, a place that seemed to meet all the criteria.

The island of New Guinea was nestled in the Pacific Ocean, eighty miles north of Australia. The second largest island of the world, it ranked next to Greenland in size. Dutch New Guinea occupied the western portion of that island and had been called *"the land that time forgot."* The eastern half of the island was governed by Australia at that time, while the western half was administered by the Dutch government. There were unexplored regions, countless tribes and villages and a variety of different languages. Many of the natives were said to be savage and cannibalistic. Tribes and villages who had never heard the Gospel and where there was as yet no written language abounded. Disease was rampant and life expectancy was short.

Not all the foreign mission agencies I checked on worked in New Guinea. The mission board that I had planned to contact the previous May did work in New Guinea and it was a good organization, but I no longer felt inclined to write to them.

In looking through a yearbook from Dallas Theological Seminary, an ad from TEAM (The Evangelical Alliance Mission) caught my attention. TEAM was an interdenominational faith mission based in Chicago, Illinois. As I recall, the ad said something like *"The day of pioneer missions is not over!"* I wondered, *"Of what does their pioneer mission work consist?"* I also pondered how much a single girl could do in pioneer work.

After considering several missionary organizations and seeking counsel, particularly from professor and former missionary Paul Davidson with whom I worked in the school office, a decision was reached. I would apply to The Evangelical Alliance Mission. In response to my inquiry, TEAM sent what they called Preliminary Information forms. Preliminary information was required before formal application forms for missionary service could be obtained. I completed and returned the forms to their office in November, 1960.

The end of November and first of December brought a missionary conference to the college. A number of speakers representing various missionary organizations participated, including Dr. Delbert Kuehl. Dr. Kuehl was a former missionary in Japan and at that time served as Candidate Secretary for TEAM.

During the meetings Dr. Kuehl showed an interesting missionary film on New Guinea and there was also an opportunity to talk privately with him. As we sat in the back of the chapel discussing my possible service with TEAM and talking about Dutch New Guinea, Dr. Kuehl frankly brought to my attention an important fact: if I went to New Guinea I would very possibly eliminate all my opportunities for marriage. There were not many eligible men running around in the jungle, he said! This was a significant reality for a young woman to face, perhaps especially for a young woman whose dream had at one time been to become a wife and mother. Here was a matter that must be given serious consideration. Jesus Himself said that we should not leap into things without counting the cost (Luke 14:25-33).

When the cost has been counted and our decision made, we are not to look back (Luke 9:62).

The response of a heart which God had filled with a passionate love for Himself was simply, *"If God wants me to be married, He can bring us together wherever I am."*

Dr. Kuehl was a great help and encouragement and I thought, *"If all the men in this Mission are like this one, this is the Mission for me."*

There was another potential obstacle – my financial situation. I had worked as much as I possibly could and carried a full load of studies. But quite a bit of money was still needed to cover the balance due on my loan from the school, room and board, dental work, medical bills, bookstore bill, and some other expenses, including transportation to and from TEAM's Candidate School if I was to attend the following June.

Apart from a $5.00 gift designated for a specific purpose, I had a total of 39 cents in my possession.

CANDIDATE SCHOOL

Chapter 13

A soft rain was gently falling as the train arrived in Chicago on a Monday night in June 1961. Lorene had also applied to TEAM and we traveled together from Memphis to attend the mission's candidate school. Near the train station we located a small restaurant, where we had supper, and then we returned to the train station to pick up our baggage and take a taxi to TEAM's international headquarters on McLean Street in Chicago.

As the school year had drawn to a close at Mid-South Bible College, my financial situation seemed to indicate that it would be necessary for me to work full time for a while before moving on toward foreign missionary service. But as I prayed and thought about what to do, I was called into the school office and given some good news. Friends wanted to underwrite the balance of my school loan!

Those who wanted to help me were not wealthy. Rather, they simply loved the Lord and had a heart for missions. One couple promised to make a monthly payment on my account until half of the debt was paid, and they had recruited another couple to pay the other half! God had wonderfully cleared the way and now I was headed for candidate school. Candidate school was a time to learn more about The Evangelical Alliance Mission (TEAM) and for TEAM to learn more about me.

The next morning, after breakfast at a grill close to the TEAM office, we joined the TEAM staff at the headquarters office for their daily 8:30 a.m. prayer meeting. Afterward we were taken to a college where candidate school would be held, and after registering we learned about the responsibilities assigned to us. Mine was to serve as clerk (secretarial post) and Lorene's was to serve as snack shop chairman.

During the ensuing weeks we attended classes where we studied about the mission's founding, administrative procedures, travel arrangements, writing missionary prayer letters and the various fields of service. Times of fellowship and making new friends were mixed with times of instruction and examination. According to my journal, on June 21, *"they gave us a whopper of an exam covering general Bible knowledge, theology, church and missionary history!"* We were also given a language aptitude examination. We gave our testimonies to the Board of Directors and were interviewed by the medical director regarding our physical and psychological health and by the doctrinal committee regarding our doctrinal position. Films presenting the missionary work in various countries were shown.

Classes related to each of the world areas where TEAM served were arranged so that candidates could gain more specific details about the work and personally meet with missionaries who had served there. Naturally I signed up for the New Guinea group.

The instructor was a tall, dark-haired young man in his early 30's from North Carolina. His name was Robert Frazier. After graduating from Bob Jones University, Bob had been ordained as a Baptist minister and gained some experience pastoring a church in this country before going overseas. He and his wife Doris had successfully completed their first term of missionary service with TEAM in New Guinea. They were on furlough and I drank in their every word. I could not have imagined in my wildest dreams what an important role Bob would play in my life in years to come!

Though we had a full schedule, not all of our time was given to study and caring for responsibilities. One evening a few of us had an impromptu party. Some of the unmarried guys invited a few of us single gals into the boys' dorm. We were served peanut butter sandwiches while one of the men with acting experience performed a scene from "Romeo and Juliet." Although it was all innocent fun, in later years I have wondered what the administration would have thought had they found a group of girls in the boys' dorm in a semi-lighted room with "Juliet" standing on top of a chest of drawers. Several missionary careers might have ended right there!

Before long the mixture of fun, inspiration,

important interviews, examinations, fellowship, soaking in of new information and getting to know new people — the things of which candidate school consisted — drew to a close. Again it was time to say goodbye to a special group of people and to a once-in-a-lifetime experience.

"Like a River Glorious is God's Perfect Peace" sounded forth from our hearts as we sang, beginning our final day together.

Then once more we sang the song which had become so much a part of our summer, *"We Rest On Thee, Our Shield and Our Defender."*

In his parting message, Dr. Kuehl left us with a promise from Isaiah 58:11, *"And the Lord shall guide thee continually, and satisfy thy soul in drought, and make fat thy bones: and thou shalt be like a watered garden, and like a spring of water, whose waters fail not."*

Dr. Johnson, the General Director, chose as his parting words 2 Corinthians 13:11, *"Finally, brethren, farewell. Be perfect, be of good comfort, be of one mind, live in peace; and the God of love and peace shall be with you."*

Then came the big moment, the culmination of the summer, when we were given individual letters from the Board of Directors. Opening mine with care, I read the thrilling words which told me that I was approved by TEAM for missionary service in Dutch New Guinea!

CALIFORNIA

Chapter 14

Immediately after the completion of candidate school in the Chicago area, I returned to Memphis and resumed employment at the college. The income from this helped to pay debts to the hospital and doctor and also covered some other miscellaneous expenses.

Now that I had been approved for missionary service with TEAM in New Guinea, my next destination was California! Sometimes there seems a fine line between faith and presumption. If we insist on doing something – simply because we want to do it and with the mistaken belief that God will make it happen if we can just work up enough faith— we may be practicing presumption. On the other hand, there *are* times when God's leading is so clear and unmistakable that we know we must do a certain thing whether or not it seems logical. This was one of those times.

I felt that the Lord had given me perfect peace

about attending Biola School of Missionary Medicine in Los Angeles, California, and the school had accepted me as a student. TEAM had approved this step of further preparation for missionary service. As yet, however, I had no money for transportation from Tennessee to California and no funds with which to begin school or to pay for books or room and board after arrival. Was God really leading me to do this? And was He leading me to do it at this time? I felt certain that He was. I was also certain that when He guides He provides, and it was my conviction that it was not necessary to tell others of my need. God Himself would provide in His own way and in His own time, and so I moved ahead with plans to go.

Matters were complicated a little more when I received word from Biola that the opening date for the School of Missionary Medicine had been rescheduled. Classes were to begin about a week earlier than originally planned. This meant quitting my job earlier and thus losing a week's salary in Memphis. On top of that, I needed to buy new eye glasses. These events drastically changed my plans for saving some money. Time moved on, but my financial situation did not improve. Less than a week remained before my scheduled departure and still the funds were not in hand.

God was not taken by surprise, however. He had known all along when school would begin and He was moving right on schedule! Soon a financial gift specifically designated for my trip was received, enough to pay half the cost of a bus ticket to Los Angeles.. A few days later, I was given another gift and it amounted to a fourth of the total cost. Now I had three fourths of the money needed. The final day before I was to leave Memphis rolled around and the last fourth was received! It came from my parents. They did not know my specific need, but I had borrowed some money from them to pay on my hospital bill and when I repaid them they sent it back to me. So there I was, the day before time to begin my journey to California, with all the money I needed to buy a ticket! Now all I needed was money to register at the school, money to buy books and money for a room and for food in Los Angeles.

That same night, the very night before my departure, I was in my apartment finishing up my packing when there was a knock at the door. Opening it, I found a couple of fellow students from MSBC standing there and when I invited them in suddenly a stream of MSBC friends poured through the doorway singing "Send the Light!" They were loaded with beautifully wrapped packages!

We had a wonderful time together, and when they had gone I found myself laden with useful gifts plus about $20 in cash. The next day, my last in Memphis, a friend who had not been at my apartment the night before gave me another $10 in cash. So I left Memphis on schedule, not only able to pay the busfare but also with $30 in hand for other needs!

On the way to California, I had the opportunity of visiting with my family in Arkansas for a few days. While there, my parents gave me several things they felt that I would need, as well as some money for food, even though I had not told them that

I lacked anything..

A few days later I stepped off the bus in another large city where I had never been before – Los Angeles — alone and yet not alone. God had provided sufficient funds for a month's rent in the dorm and to buy food for several days. I was also able to have my watch repaired, a necessity for medical training. But the Lord was by no means finished!

Sometimes it seems easier to look back at such thrilling experiences and rejoice in how God worked so wonderfully than it is to go through them at the time! God had been so faithful and I was thoroughly convinced that I was following His leading. Yet human nature being what it is, as I approached the registration desk at the School of Missionary Medicine to register without the required funds, there was a certain amount of trepidation in my heart. My turn came to stand in front of the lady who was registering the students and collecting fees and to tell her that I didn't yet have the money. With an expression on her face that I could not quite interpret, she said *"I think you'd better talk with the dean!"*

My trepidation and I were escorted to the office of the dean, where for the first time I met the Dean of Biola School of Missionary Medicine, Leonie Soubirou. Miss Soubirou, a tall in-charge looking woman graciously invited me to sit down. Then she listened attentively to my story and when I finished simply said, *"Would you like a job?"* *"I'd love a job!"* I responded gratefully and enthusiastically. God had done it again! The following day, Saturday, September 2, 1961, I began working in the office of the Biola School of Missionary Medicine, officially a student and ready to begin classes.

Life in California settled down to a routine of work and study. Before long, our uniforms were issued and then the new and interesting dimension of hospital duty was added to our days in the classroom and practice lab. Student uniforms for the women consisted of white jumpers with pink blouses and white nurses caps, and the men wore white shirts, white trousers and a bow tie. Hospital affiliation at Shriner's Hospital for Crippled Children and at Hollywood Presbyterian Hospital brought challenging and interesting training.

The School of Missionary Medicine was located in downtown Los Angeles, on Hope Street. Part of the fourteen story building was used for classes and part for dorm rooms. Classrooms and offices occupied the ninth floor of Stewart Hall, and the chapel and kitchen were next to each other on the seventh floor. Missionary med students shared the kitchen. There was also a school cafeteria in the basement area. I lived on the sixth floor. Students were assigned small individual rooms and each floor had a bathroom at the end of a long hall. Biola was in the process of building a new campus at La Mirada, California, and many of the college students already lived out there. However, some still lived in the downtown buildings, with bus transportation to and from the new campus provided by the college. Those of us in the medical school traveled to and from the hospitals with students who had cars, sharing transportation costs.

A dilemma of a different sort developed when a

young man, a committed Christian who was also planning to be a missionary, felt that he was in love with me. For a while I was in a quandary as I struggled with my own feelings and sought to know what God wanted me to do. Through these times God was able to teach me more about myself and more of Himself.

How I wish I had a more complete record of God's marvelous provision during those days. However, the pressures of work, school, homework, hospital and church activities absorbed time and strength and left little of either for recording daily events.

A small church about a mile's walk from the school, Eleventh Street Baptist Church, became my church family. What a precious group it was. Fellowship still continues with some of them, at least by correspondence or e-mail, even though the church itself was dissolved years ago. The city needed the property, and the church membership dispersed to other churches.

Life was busy in California, but thought also had to be given to future plans and next steps. My next destination would be the University of Oklahoma at Norman!

OKLAHOMA

Chapter 15

One of the requirements for missionary service with TEAM in New Guinea was training in linguistics. Wycliffe Bible Translators offered a summer course in linguistics at several universities, and I chose the University of Oklahoma at Norman. It was closest to my home in Arkansas. Since the course was offered only during the summer, it was necessary to request a leave of absence from my medical studies.

A few other students were also going to various universities for the summer. We went through a graduation ceremony at Biola in the spring of 1962, but still needed to return in the fall and complete the final semester of the medical course before we would actually be considered graduates. After that, we could exchange our blank papers for real diplomas and then take the California State Board nursing examinations.

So it was that once again I found myself headed

for another state and another school with no money – either for the journey to Oklahoma, back to California or for university expenses.

Several journal entries recorded a now familiar experience. On April 4, 1962, I wrote,

> *"Yesterday the application to the Wycliffe Bible Translators Summer Institute of Linguistics was placed in the mail . . . I did not have – and would not have been able to work into my budget – the required $15 application fee. But several days ago, I awoke one morning to find that a plain envelope containing $15 had been slipped under my door."*

And on April 14, 1962,

> *"Received letter of acceptance yesterday from Wycliffe . . . No money in sight yet for paying off everything here and transportation to and expenses while in Oklahoma."*

May 28, 1962,

> *"Less than a week till time to leave for SIL at Norman. Source of transportation money and money for the course still unknown. "Father, You know what You are doing. 'Grant me patience and wisdom, I pray'."*

On June 13, 1962, I was able to report,

> *"Today begins my second day of classes at SIL. The last week before time to leave*

California rolled around and still no money. Only a couple of days remained. The Lord arranged a ride with two others, which would be much less than busfare and He provided that much money. Registration . . . the hour I dreaded had come – facing those in charge without sufficient finances for the course. By this time the Lord had provided $30 to pay on it, but this was still a long way from paying all I would owe. However, as I told them I could not pay it all and how much I could pay, they accepted it without a word and I was registered! Praise the Lord . . . He will provide the remainder of the funds in His own way and time."

By late July I was not only dealing with linguistic classes, but also with some anxiety. I questioned myself about whether or not I should have done something differently. On July 25, 1962, I wrote,

"No money has come to pay the rest of my School of Missionary Medicine bill or my bill here and as each day passed and still it has not come, my heart has grown more and more frantic. I did not even realize this – perhaps I didn't want to believe such a thing about myself. But it was true. It was not really that I doubted God's faithfulness, but I felt that I have possibly failed in the proper handling of funds. . . But regardless of what has put me in the situation, He caused me to realize my need to cast it <u>all</u> upon Him. So I

cried unto Him . . . Accepting His cleansing by faith – not feeling – I very soon had assurance that He had heard . . . He is going to provide!"

August 11, 1962,

"This has been quite a summer, one filled with many battles . . . Yesterday, when I returned to my room after lunch, there was an envelope lying on my desk. These words were written on the front of it: 'This won't take you all the way to New Guinea, but it might help on the way to California."

God had not failed. He was returning me to California to complete my medical studies.

On September 22, 1962, my journal continued,

"The Lord did bring me back to California – providing transportation, a place to live and grocery money. We have been here four happy weeks. Sherry joined us at the end of the first week, so now there are four of us (Sherry Archibald, Sue Risley, Joy Oram and myself)."

Instead of living in the dormitory for the final semester, the four of us shared a little house on a hillside in Glendale, California.

Those final weeks were happy ones for all of us. We divided up the household responsibilities, rotating on a weekly basis: 1) grocery shopping and cooking meals, 2) washing dishes, 3) laundry and 4) house-cleaning. We agreed on a budget and each of us gave our money to the one who was in charge of cooking for the week. As we sometimes had unexpected guests for the main meal in the evening, we learned to plan meals that could be shared beyond the four of us without a problem. The guys who dropped by occasionally and had an evening meal with us sometimes brought along some meat to add to our supplies and that helped keep us within our budget.

Eventually our studies were finished and California State Board nursing examinations were successfully completed, but because of some medical problems I was not allowed to proceed immediately with overseas plans.

On Friday, October 19, 1962, I recorded,

> *"Today is our last day as missionary med students – our last day of white pinafores and pink blouses and the security of having the name 'student' to help excuse our mistakes!*
>
> *Very literally, this morning, 'I know not what the future holds,' but am so glad that also 'I know Who holds the future, and He Who holds the future holds my hand.' The Lord has shown that I should stay here – at least temporarily – but how long and what to do has yet to be known to me. Medical advice was to stay until my present physical condition is straightened out. But should I work, and where, or plan deputation, and where, or*

both, or something else?"

A short time later, Sue and I obtained employment at the Los Angeles County General Hospital where I worked as a nurse in the neurosurgical intensive care unit until the end of December. When I applied for the job I told them that I could only work there for two months.

On November 14, 1962, my journal entry describes a time of searching and decision making,

> *" . . . Really just two months? To work longer would mean being able to save more, which could be used in getting me to the field. But no. As of today, I feel that what He said to me that first day – so clearly I almost missed it – is what He wants, only two months."*

My goals were: Return to Arkansas and spend some time with my parents, then go to Memphis and care for Lorene through her surgery in January, do deputation work in the Memphis area and plan my departure for New Guinea in March 1963.

> Some very personal musings and soul searching were recorded on November 21, 1962, *"Big oaks from little acorns grow. How very true. And it is not only a principle found true in the realm of acorns and oaks. Satan knows we – when we are walking close by our Lord – are not apt to fall prey to him. But rather, how wisely he plants a little here, then adds a little there, until one morning we*

wake up and find our spiritual coldness the size of a great oak.

"As I look back, I think how very easy some physical trials have been, because with them there was an abounding joy in the sense of God's presence and the comforting assurance that this was what He wanted to use to work out His will in me. How foolish I am to think that all our testings would or should be the same. Our dear heavenly Father wants us to <u>grow</u>. I have found myself wincing and questioning and almost fainting beneath the tests and disciplines of spiritual and mental and emotional conflicts. No, often – and perhaps most of the time –others are not standing by to give us gifts expressing thoughtfulness and concern, or saying a comforting word, or helping in some other way, because they cannot see these things as they can see our physical wounds, nor know our need of their help.

"But it seems that now God says, 'Those things were <u>primer</u> level. They were not easy the first time. Remember when you cried out, 'why did this have to happen to <u>me</u>?' " No, we must not expect to ever reach a level where we have attained (in this life). When we have learned God's primer level lessons, He has advanced ones for us. Should we give up then in the face of ever facing new disciplines? No! We must only yield ourselves the more fully to Him, knowing that He 'is able

to make all grace abound toward you,' that
we may have 'all sufficiency in all things.' 2
Corinthians 9:8.

"In my flesh, I would desire to stay at the
primer level. There I have found God sufficient, there I have experienced His grace.
'Oh God, give grace to trust Thee – and lead
on to the advanced level, where Thy perfect
and complete will might be wrought in this
life that You desire to conform to the image
of Your Son!' "

My time in California was drawing to a close
and on December 13, 1962, I wrote,

"Today is Thursday. The days are passing
quickly and the time of my departure from Los
Angeles is not far away now. Monday night it
was our joy to have four of our faculty
members from the School of Missionary
Medicine over for dinner and a time of fellowship – Leonie Soubirou, Eunice Jones, Ruth
Fuller and Leta Kilander. The Lord gave
another tremendous blessing that evening
about an hour before they arrived. I was in the
kitchen preparing Southern fried chicken
when the telephone rang. Sue answered and it
was long distance for me. It was Dr. James
Crichton, president of Mid-South Bible
College, asking me to come to work part time
in the college bookstore while doing deputation in the Memphis area. Another answer to
prayer and another assurance that I have

planned according to His will! Also, the hours are good, 9:00 - 1:00, so that it is not too early in case I have been out speaking the night before and I am off early to finish getting ready for another evening engagement."

My final entry for that year was recorded on December 27, 1962,

"This morning has dawned bright and clear, my last here in Glendale. From where I am sitting on the couch, the mountains are in clear view and beautiful. Palm trees are standing serenely, and occasionally a bird flitters through the sky. In our yard, there are two pretty cats. This has been a wonderful year and in a way I hate to see it draw to a close. But at the same time I am thrilled that the Lord is moving me along to do His will and anticipating (perhaps with a little fear and trembling) the future."

DISCOURAGEMENT

Chapter 16

The future that I had anticipated with "fear and trembling" was soon upon me! The years of schooling were past and a new phase of life was beginning.

It was January, 1963, and my next aspiration was to arrive in New Guinea by spring, before the country changed governments and visas became more difficult to obtain. I knew it was a big goal, but felt that somehow God would very possibly accomplish it. Plans for a March departure meant that I would need several thousand dollars by February. That did not include the expense of necessary dental work, purchase and packing of clothes and supplies for the field, immunizations and miscellaneous. But God was able! In January the first two promises of financial support for missionary service were made.

Then came the blow narrated in my journal on January 28, 1963.

"One week ago tonight I received a letter

> *from TEAM's Medical Director containing a*
> *message that could change my whole future.*
> *He felt I should consider a field (South*
> *Africa), where medical help (doctors, etc.)*
> *would be available to me. Change fields?*
> *And right in the middle of deputation?"*

I had never been considered a robust individual and there had always been the question of my being able to obtain medical clearance for service in New Guinea, but I thought that had been settled. Earlier I had asked my doctor in Memphis exactly what problem I had that might prevent my going to New Guinea as a missionary. He explained, *"It's just that you are not what we consider a physically strong person and I'm afraid you couldn't survive in the jungle."* Nevertheless, when he saw my strong conviction that God wanted me to go to New Guinea, eventually he recommended medical clearance. He was a committed Christian physician who served on the Board of Directors of Mid-South Bible College.

The January 28 entry continued,

> *" At first, I just couldn't believe it! But as*
> *the reality of the matter penetrated my mind,*
> *I could only turn to Him Who had called me*
> *and yield afresh to go <u>anywhere</u> He wants.*
> *Though I was confused and knew not which*
> *way to turn, He knows and not only knows*
> *but <u>controls</u> the future."*

Yet I felt so sure God was going to open the way

for me to go to West Irian that I moved ahead with plans and preparation to go. Presumption or ignorance? I'm not sure. During that time I was sharing an apartment with Lorene in Memphis and seeking to be of help to her as she underwent surgery in February and again in early March.

The days passed and my plans began to look more and more impossible. My heart was heavy, as my feelings portrayed in my March 9, 1963, journal entry.

> *"There is certainly a temptation to frustration when I strain my eyes (spiritually) to see into the future. What I have felt was God's leading looks more and more impossible. I hardly know how to plan even for the immediate future just now . . . 'Oh, Father, my faith is so weak . . .' "*

On April 7, 1963, I wrote

> *"This is April – no visa applied for, support not in, passage and equipment still lacking, an almost $400 dental bill to be paid, and a doctor bill with more coming up for the four injections yet to be taken, and a couple or so of lesser bills. . ."*

Discouragement and confusion flourished as I wrote on April 17, 1963,

> *"Oh Dear God, my Father, I fall before Thee today with a heavy heart. It seems tears would help, but they do not come. How I had hoped that <u>today</u> would be the day the letter*

from the Mission would come. Time is so short and the passing of each day seems to lessen the possibility of my going to New Guinea with those who are to be there before May 1. . . I have done all I know to do; passport is in hand, family has been notified, school (employment) has been notified, dental work has been completed and all immunizations are completed except the final two that are due in just a few days. . . I thought You wanted me in New Guinea, and that You wanted me to go in April. . . I pray not that You will send me to New Guinea, but that You will accomplish your perfect will, whatever it is."

Like Abraham awaiting the birth of Isaac, I did not understand that several years would lie between the call and the fulfillment. God had a lot to do in my life before I reached New Guinea.

DISAPPOINTMENT

Chapter 17

I have heard it said many times that disappointments are sometimes God's appointments.

With my hopes for getting to West Irian in April dashed, the end of May 1963 found me again in Los Angeles, a weary and confused young woman. Unlike my previous experiences of clear leading, great peace and miraculous provision, now I seemed to have no peace in any direction. Uncertain about what to do, but feeling I must do something, I returned to California.

On arrival back in Los Angeles, I stopped by the School of Missionary Medicine for a visit and Miss Soubirou immediately invited me to return to work in her office. She told me that if I had not been called to go overseas she would have encouraged me to go into administration as a profession. However, her heart and her ministry in the Biola School of Missionary Medicine were deeply committed to missions and she did not want to discourage me from my continued efforts to serve overseas. I enjoyed working with her and she was a great influence on my life.

On Sunday, June 9, 1963, I wrote in my journal,

> " . . . *I had thought that surely the Lord wanted me to leave for New Guinea in April. I was so sure of it that plans beyond that, as far as what to do if I didn't go then, seemed to be a lack of faith. . . . When word came out that all those who were ready, as far as schooling, etc., were to be sent out, even without sufficient funds, in April, due to the governmental changeover on May 1, I knew that this must be how God was going to do it. . . But as day after day passed, I finally realized and had to face the fact that I was not getting to go in April . . . Medical clearance finally came, but not until too late in April to get to go. It was too late to get a visa."*

Although it was disappointing not to be going overseas as soon as I had hoped and planned, being back in Los Angeles brought many blessings. The ladies I worked with in the school office were a source of daily fellowship and encouragement, and I had the opportunity of getting acquainted with another class of School of Missionary Medicine students. It was also good to be back in the Eleventh Street Baptist Church family.

When in August and September of 1963, a Billy Graham Crusade came to Los Angeles, I had the privilege of serving as a counselor and singing in the choir. The beautiful old hymn *"Blessed Assurance"* sounded forth in the Los Angeles Coliseum as the dedication service for workers opened on the evening of August 14, 1963. Dr. Graham's message to us was based on Romans 12 and 2 Chronicles 6 and 7 as he challenged all of us to examine our own hearts and to offer ourselves afresh in dedication to God and for His use. The crusade officially opened the next evening, on August 15, and I truly witnessed a work of the Spirit of God in the service. There were no emotional appeals and no pressure, but when an invitation was given people poured into the aisles. I was glad that I could participate every single night until it concluded on September 8. In addition to Billy Graham's messages, I was blessed by the ministries of others on the platform — Charles E. Fuller of the "Old Fashioned Revival Hour," Dr. V. Raymond Edman of Wheaton, IL, and the music of George Beverly Shea and Ethel Waters among others. On the closing night, the Los Angeles Coliseum was packed to overflowing with an estimated overflow of 20,000 people still outside. After the closing invitation, the choir sang the "Hallelujah Chorus" followed by "Turn Your Eyes Upon Jesus" as the great crowd was leaving.

The next entry in my journal was on September 12 1963, when a call on the hall phone (we did not have individual phones in our rooms) summoned me as I was finishing my shower.

> *". . . When I learned it was long distance for a moment the anticipation of bad news crossed my mind until what cheery voice*

*should come over the wire but Lorene's. It
was wonderful to hear her voice and for the
next few <u>minutes</u> we tried to cram in several
<u>hours</u> of talking. . . . Since I have been
informed that it may be up to two and a half
years before a visa can be secured for West
Irian (Dutch New Guinea's new name) –
though I have kept hoping it would be less – I
was somewhat startled by her question,
'Helen, if it takes two years, will you wait?'
To my mind the answer came immediately,
'What else can I do but wait?'*

Her reason for asking was that she wanted to
discuss the idea of our enrolling in a two-year graduate course in missions at another school. I gave it
some serious thought and prayer, but in the end
neither of us enrolled in it.

I continued to work at the Biola School of
Missionary Medicine in Los Angeles and Lorene
continued to manage the college bookstore at Mid-
South Bible College in Memphis. That was a position
she had been given prior to graduation from college
and to which she returned following candidate school
in Chicago. Although Lorene was approved for
service overseas with TEAM, she had been delayed
by orthopedic problems and multiple surgeries.

October 14, 1963, found me writing,

*"If during these months of delay (seem-
ingly – to human eyes), this time of waiting
day after day for some word that will affect*

the future, nothing is accomplished other than my learning to wait on the Lord and to walk step by step with Him, they will not have been wasted."

God continued to supply my needs. An October 15 entry reminds me of one such incidence.

"I desperately needed a pair of shoes for work and church. I had been postponing buying things that would be of use only in this country and used my income for expenses and to continue paying off medical and dental bills, etc. Then I fell and broke off the heel of one shoe of my only decent pair of shoes. Knowing I must get another pair, I went to my room and was counting to see how much money I could get together. I turned and behind me a few feet away on the floor by the door was a white envelope. *Opening it, I found enough cash to supplement the lack and a note saying, 'A gift from Him! Use it where it's most needed.' Isaiah 30:18."*

This was a special blessing to me in that since I had finished school and was working full time, it seemed that probably no one would suspect that I had a financial need. But <u>God</u> knew and He had laid it on someone's heart to help me! In addition to supplying my need, God had allowed this to happen on an evening when the stores in downtown Los Angeles would be open late enough for me to shop. As I recall, during that period of time the department stores were open late only one night each week.

About seven months after my return to Los Angeles, the long desired visa application for West Irian reached me on December 23, 1963. At last something was happening!

The exciting task of collecting and preparing the required documents took about a month. Then at last, on January 24, 1964, the visa application papers for entry into West Irian were placed in the mail and my last day of employment at Biola was set for February 1, 1964.

But things were not to move ahead as smoothly or as quickly as I had hoped. On that very date — February 1— my last day of employment at Biola School of Missionary Medicine, a letter arrived from TEAM informing me that my visa application had been put on hold! This was due to the government's refusal of visas to other applicants. Miss Soubirou invited me to stay on and work with her for another week. That would give me a few days to recoup from the disappointment and decide what to do next. Then, the day before that week was up, she asked me to stay indefinitely.

The months passed and February turned into June. The clouds lifted and I began to sense that God wanted me to leave Los Angeles in August. After the long period of waiting, I now felt that He had given me a clear, definite and settled peace about planning my departure from California on August 1. I had been invited to serve at the TEAM headquarters office in Chicago, beginning in September, after spending some time in deputation during August.

A letter came from Lorene, who was still managing the college book store, in which she mentioned as a bit of news that the housemother would not be returning to Mid-South Bible College in the fall. She wrote something like this, *"We don't know who is going to take her place."* As I read those lines, it seemed that the Lord said to my heart, *"You are!"* I thought, *"But Lord, how can that be? I'm scheduled to begin working in Chicago in September."* It was so clear, however, that I began to watch the mail for a letter from Dr. Crichton, the college president. None came.

What did happen next was that a letter came from the TEAM's administrative secretary, saying that the person whose place I was to take would be staying until November. He felt that perhaps I could continue working at Biola School of Missionary Medicine until the end of October, instead of the end of July.

However, the Lord's guidance that I should leave on August 1 had seemed very clear. I continued to seek His will and found no indication that He wanted me to change these plans. As for being a housemother at Mid-South Bible College, after a period of time had passed and I had received no word from anyone about it (neither had I mentioned it to anyone), I more or less decided that it was probably just my imagination and not really the Lord at all! I must simply go ahead and take the one step that was clear, that of leaving Los Angeles on August 1, 1964, and then trust Him to show me the next step when His time came. He had been teaching me the value of waiting on Him and He would not let me down, even if I had to wait until the last minute for His guidance.

I had not been impressed in the least that I should write and ask about the position at MSBC. Since I was waiting for a visa and planning to depart for West Irian when it came, the services I could offer anywhere in the meantime were rather indefinite. I had planned to go to the Memphis area for some speaking engagements and so moved ahead in that direction.

After leaving California on August 1 and then spending some time at home with my parents in Arkansas, I arrived in Memphis on Friday night, August 14, 1964. My journal entry reads

> *"Coming here was the last step of what I felt to be the Lord's <u>revealed</u> will for me. I was very tired and quite discouraged."*

Then the following Monday morning, Dr. Crichton telephoned me at the apartment where I was staying with Lorene and her roommate, Jimmie Gail Gourd. He asked if I could come by his office, and the Lord reminded me of what He had told me almost two months before!

That afternoon I sat in Dr. Crichton's office and he began to tell me about the difficulty they were facing in securing a housemother for the new school year which would begin in less than a month. Various ladies had been considered, but in each case it had not worked out for one reason or another. I listened while he told me the story of their need.

Then I began to tell him how the Lord had been leading me (which until then had been kept solely between the Lord and myself). I accepted the position for the time I expected to be available and then Dr. Crichton called in the dean, Roger Clapp, and shared the news with him. We all rejoiced together in the marvelous ways of the Lord and had prayer.

The commitment to serve as housemother was only temporary, due to my plans to begin working in Chicago with TEAM in November, but it would give them a little more time to look for someone to fill the post on a longer term basis. It was also with the understanding that whenever the Lord sent my visa I would be free to go.

Thus on September 1, 1964, exactly one month from the day I left Los Angeles, I officially joined the staff of Mid-South Bible College.

My life's journey certainly seemed to be following a circuitous route!

DELAY

Chapter 18

Although I had assisted the housemother during my senior year of college, actually being the housemother was a new experience. What a wonderful time it was working with young people who shared my commitment to the Lord as they studied and sought God's plan for their lives. By then I was 29 years old, almost 30, but felt a little young and inexperienced to be the *"mother"* of college students! Lorene visited the dorm and told the girls, *"Don't think you can get away with anything. Helen's already done it all! You can't hide anything from her!"* I pinned my long hair up on my head in an attempt to appear more mature.

Another month passed and then came the next shock. On October 2, 1964, I was stunned by a message from the mission and wrote of my feelings, *"Tonight I am somewhat numb in the news that has reached me today: visa refused!"* Indonesia was not granting visas to American citizens at that time.

After three years of waiting, I had again run into a dead end.

Numb with disappointment and disbelief, my heart was heavy. My journal continued ,

> *"Dear God, I love You and trust You and my heart is comforted in the realization that Your love for me is even greater. I do not understand every step that is necessary in the fulfilling of Your will, but You have granted enough understanding that I know it is right if You have allowed it or caused it to come about. Thank you for this."*

What now? For one thing, life in the dorm moved on. MSBC and TEAM had worked out an agreement for me to remain at my post in the college until the school closed for Christmas. I was scheduled to arrive in Chicago on December 30, and begin working at TEAM headquarters on January 4, 1965. Would the denial of my visa for West Irian change things?

After my visa was refused, the college asked me to consider continuing as housemother for the remainder of the school year. Then Pastor Johnson, my pastor in Los Angeles, sent a special delivery letter urging me to pray about returning to the Eleventh Street Baptist Church, where I could serve as church secretary and also have a ministry with ladies. Torn between three opportunities – the college in Memphis, the mission headquarters office in Chicago, and the church in Los Angeles – all of which were desirable — I wondered and prayed about what I should do. Finally I reached the decision that I should stay on course with my previous plans for going to Chicago and working in the TEAM office.

December was filled with many things. A final physical checkup on December 16 was followed by admission to a Memphis hospital on the 17th, minor surgery on the 18th, a return to Lorene and Jimmie Gail's apartment on the 19th and then home to Fort Smith on the 20th.

Returning to Memphis on December 28, I completed my work at MSBC on the 29th and also finished packing for the move to Chicago. Lorene accompanied me on the train trip to Chicago and we left Memphis on December 30. With her help, I spent New Year's Day 1965 in Chicago packing a container to be shipped overseas. Then Lorene returned home to Memphis, and I began work in the TEAM headquarters office on January 4, 1965.

January and February rolled by. The world situation was such that there was no hope in sight for getting more missionaries into West Irian, at least not in the foreseeable future. As a result, TEAM asked me to think about serving in some other area of the world, at least on a temporary basis. God's call to serve in West Irian had seemed so definite. Choose another field? How could I?

After years of feeling that God was leading me to serve in West Irian and years of waiting for that door to open, considering another field seemed strange. Still somewhat bewildered, and almost feeling unfaithful, I began to prayerfully study the brochures about other countries where TEAM worked. I was looking for a place that in some ways came closest to West

Irian. Maybe God did want me to serve somewhere other than West Irian, at least on a temporary basis.

On March 24, 1965, a settled peace came to my heart about serving in Rhodesia (now Zimbabwe) if God opened the way. Rhodesia was nestled deep in the heart of Africa, south of the Congo and north of South Africa. A well known missionary of years past, David Livingstone, had been there.

I earnestly asked God to open or close the way so that His plan would be worked out in my life. It might be confusing to me, but it was clear to Him. The following day I talked with Dr. Kuehl, TEAM's candidate secretary, regarding my decision and requested visa application papers for Rhodesia.

Unlike my repeated attempts to go to West Irian and the repeated closing of doors, as I prepared to go to Africa the doors started to swing open fast enough to make my head swim! Again I set about preparing documents required for a visa application. The required police clearance from Los Angeles was received, my other forms added, and the visa application was submitted by TEAM on April 13, 1965 — less than three weeks after the decision was made. Expecting no problems in obtaining the visa, the Mission made tentative plans for my departure from New York by air on June 15.

On June 2, 1965, I finished packing containers for my shipment to Africa and then left Chicago for Arkansas and a last visit with my parents before leaving the country. My mom had recently had surgery and came home from the hospital the day I arrived. Her surgeon told me that she would be fine; there was no need to delay my plans. On June 9, 1965, my commissioning service was conducted at Willow Park Baptist Church in Memphis, Tennessee.

What a wonderful evening of fellowship and blessing it was, as I gathered with friends from school and the church. My beloved professor and former coworker, Rev. Paul Davidson, brought the message, and MSBC president, Dr. James Crichton, led in the prayer of dedication. Pastor John Seaton gave a charge to the church to stand with me in prayer and in other ways. The Willow Park Baptist Church family faithfully fulfilled that charge, supporting me financially, by prayer and in other ways during all of my years overseas.

The visa for Rhodesia, however, did not come through quite as quickly as had been anticipated, and once again I was thrust into a time of waiting. Extending my stay in Memphis, I helped Lorene in the college bookstore. That temporary job and the salary were very welcome, as by that time I was quite low on personal funds.

Then on June 22, 1965, I flew to New York City, where I stayed at the TEAM guest house in Brooklyn during my final days of waiting for a visa to enter Rhodesia. As there were no other missionaries there at that time and the hostess of the guest house did not speak a lot of English, it was somewhat a time of isolation. I used the time for study and to finish a correspondence course in Journalism. Not knowing how long I would be there, each day I went grocery shopping and spent some of the meager funds that remained in my possession to buy enough food for one more day. I was down to $5.00.

The TEAM center in Brooklyn was small and space was limited and before my visa was received, missionaries who had made previous reservations arrived from overseas and needed the room. God provided another place for me through a retired missionary widow from India, Mrs. Richard Thomas. I did not know her, but she was a retired TEAM missionary who came by the center and offered to take me home with her. I stayed in her home until time to leave for Africa. She did not know what little money I had, but even so would not take any reimbursement for my stay with her.

Finally, on July 1 the wonderful news came from TEAM headquarters in Chicago that my visa had been received! On July 7, 1965, I wrote in my journal,

> *"This is the long awaited day! It is now 3:40 p.m. Lord willing, I will be flying from Kennedy International Airport at 10:00 p.m. en route to the mission field."*

A man from the church I had visited with my missionary hostess offered to take me to the airport. It was my intention to give him my last $5 to help with his gasoline expense and to thank him for this kindness (without letting him know that was all I had, of course!). However, instead of accepting it, he handed me a gift of $20!

Thus it was that with $25 in my purse, I began my journey across the Atlantic ocean – alone, but not alone – on my way to Africa!

AFRICA

Chapter 19

"*A rrived today in paradise! My heart was so filled with gratitude that my eyes brimmed with tears as I looked about at this lovely land today. How gracious is God to send me to such a place. And how glad I am for the peace and assurance that fill my heart with the confidence that this is His will for now and that He will continue to work out in detail each subsequent step!*" So reads my diary entry for Friday, July 9, 1965, the day I arrived in Rhodesia.

Occupying a high plain that averaged between 3,000 and 5,000 feet above sea level, temperatures in Rhodesia averaged between seventy and seventy-five degrees. Of course, it was warmer in some areas and cooler in others, depending on the altitude. The Zambezi Valley could get very hot, over one hundred degrees, while the capital city of Salisbury was often cool, especially at night.

When TEAM missionaries first went to Rhodesia, in the 1940's, to begin work in the Zambezi Valley, the tribal people were their only neighbors. The African bush was alive with leopards, lions and elephants, along with other types of wild life.

In the remote rural areas, termed "*the bush*," Africans lived in round huts made of mud and covered with thatched roofs. Some used ox-drawn carts with crudely carved wooden wheels. They ground corn by pounding it with a heavy stick inside a hollowed out log. This supplied their primary staple food, *sadza,* a thick corn meal mush. Sometimes the *sadza* was accompanied by vegetables and perhaps some meat and gravy if available. Cooking was done outside, over an open fire. Water from nearby rivers or streams was carried in containers on their heads.

TEAM's multifaceted ministry in Rhodesia included a hospital in the bush which served an area larger than the state of Massachusetts. The hospital had seventy beds to care for inpatients and many more were treated as outpatients. A modern operating room and x-ray facilities were in use. Along with receiving treatment for their physical needs, the staff sought to meet their even greater need, the spiritual one. Two African evangelists worked with the patients, in addition to the efforts of the missionary staff. In the hospital's school of nursing, qualified African students were trained to become good nurses.

The Missionary Aviation Fellowship plane was based on the hospital station. Pilot Dave Voetmann and his wife Marilee maintained a very vital role in the overall missionary work.

Though Africans were hungry for education, not everyone had the opportunity of attending school.

TEAM reached out to them in this need through many elementary schools, and also provided one high school. A Bible school trained young men and women in the Bible.

Another ministry was the Bible correspondence course, which was reaching thousands. Literature, too, was an important service. The mission's publication department produced many items, from Sunday school material and Christian booklets to tracts. It was a rare thing to have an African refuse a tract. But it was very common for them to request one if they knew one was available. They were eager to read, especially in their own language.

The "Homecraft School" for African women helped them learn how to be better homemakers. They received instruction in such things as cooking, sewing and knitting, etc., along with learning more of the Bible.

In the cities, public schools conducted Bible instruction classes as a part of the curriculum and missionaries assisted the schools by helping to staff these classes. There were more opportunities of this type than there were missionaries to fill them. Each denomination was given the privilege of providing a class for the students of their faith. TEAM provided classes for those who had no church affiliation.

Other missionaries, some living in the bush and others in the cities, carried on evangelistic and church planting ministries, and also held short term Bible schools for the purpose of discipling laymen.

Almost all mission stations had a clinic, as there was much sickness.

In Hatfield, a suburb of the beautiful and modern capital city of Salisbury (now Harare), TEAM had a radio recording studio. Programs were produced in the African language for release over the Rhodesia Broadcasting Corporation.

Hatfield was also the location of a Missionary Children's Home where one of the missionary couples gave full time to caring for the school-aged children of the missionaries who lived in the bush. MK's (missionary kids) lived there during the school year, while attending public schools, and returned home to visit their parents in the bush during school holidays.

TEAM's Rhodesia headquarters, the administrative center for the field, was located in Hatfield. This became my home during my years in Rhodesia. From there, daily radio contact was maintained with all of the missionaries.

When I left New York bound for Rhodesia, I did not know what my assignment would be or where I would be stationed after language school. I simply went to do whatever I could. It turned out that there was a need for help in the field headquarters office and that became my primary assignment – part time while in language study and full time afterward. Teaching a Bible class in one of the public schools and visiting African women patients in the large government hospital in Salisbury rounded out my ministry. I had finally arrived on a foreign mission field and life in Africa had begun!

One of the first challenges ahead of me in Africa was language study. I agreed with the Mission that it was important to learn the African language, even though the national language in Rhodesia was English. The Zezuru dialect of the Shona language was the language most used by Africans in our area, though some Africans also spoke English very well.

As a woman, learning the language was especially important to me because a lot of African women could not speak English. Many were skilled in homemaking crafts, making beautiful net table cloths (used to cover food laden tables, especially outdoors), crocheted and beaded doilies and other items. Peddling them from door to door was a way they could earn some money. Other times they went door-to-door to ask if the person living there had any used clothing to sell.

The apartment complex where I lived was located about three miles from the mission office. One day two African ladies knocked on the door of my apartment with handcrafted items for sale. As I examined their wares, I began to chat with them in Shona – very haltingly. They were so thrilled that they wanted to *give* me the items they had been attempting to sell! *"You speak our language!"* they exclaimed with delight. As for me, I was delighted that they understood me and also that it made them so happy!

Along with learning a new language came the learning of a new culture and of customs that differed from my American background.

African people were usually very polite. They were careful to greet one another. It was not courteous to just say hello and immediately start talking, as we Americans do. You must not only greet the person, but if it is morning you must inquire as to how he slept and then he in turn will inquire how you slept. If it is later in the day, he will ask whether you have had a good day and you in turn must do the same before beginning to talk about something else. Three different sets of greetings were used, one in the morning, a different one around noon time, and a third in the late afternoon and evening.

I learned that when something was handed to me, it was polite to extend both hands in accepting it. If I did use only one hand, it should always be the right hand and never the left. Usually those who were especially courteous would clap their hands together first. Ladies often also made a little curtsy along with saying *"ndatenda"* ("thank you").

Age was meaningful and respected. If an African wanted to show special respect, he might call a person "grandmother" or "grandfather."

Also, because there were many British people in Rhodesia, it was likewise necessary to adjust to differences between the British and American cultures.

From the British, I learned to eat using a fork with my left hand. It turned out to be a lot more sensible than the way I'd always done it, i.e., cutting my meat, laying down the knife and transferring the fork back to my right hand. I even learned how to eat peas on the back of my fork! Among other things, I also learned to enjoy hot tea with milk in it.

Although both Americans and British spoke English, a little interpretation was necessary at times. For example, a statement like, *"My geyser packed up"* meant that the speaker's hot water tank had quit working! The hood of a car was the bonnet and the horn was a hooter. A torch was a flashlight. A hot dog was a frank. A sweater was a jersey.

There was also often a difference of pronunciation of the same word. For instance, a banana was a "ba<u>nah</u>na," a tomato was a "to<u>mah</u>to" and a potato was a "po<u>tah</u>to." A bath was a "b<u>ah</u>th." In some cases, the difference was in which syllable was accented. For example, a <u>con</u>troversy in American pronunciation was a con<u>trov</u>ersy in British English. A <u>lab</u>oratory was a la<u>bor</u>atory, and on it went. On one occasion when I placed a long distance call to a distant destination regarding a flight plan for the MAF plane, the man on the other end of the line simply could not understand my American accent. Finally he said, *"Lady, you'd better hang up and send a telegram!"*

Gradually my speech gravitated to theirs. As it did, one day I went into a store and asked for some ba<u>nah</u>-nas, and the clerk said, *"Don't you usually say bananas?"* Much, much later Dr. Mortenson, TEAM's General Director, visited Rhodesia. As he sat in the office and listened to me talk on the phone, he looked at me and said, *"Helen, you've lost your southern accent. Now you have a British accent!"* And when I first returned to America a few years later, I was asked my nationality by another American.

Learning to use money was another challenge. Instead of dollars and cents, I now shopped with pounds, shillings and pence. Before I learned to count the local currency, when I went shopping I just held out my money and said, "*Take what you need!*"

July turned into December, and December brought my first Christmas in Africa. It was a lovely day – warm and sunny. December falls during the summertime in Rhodesia. Another single missionary, Marian Wilterdink, and I went to the Chironga mission station out in the bush to spend the holidays with missionaries there.

On Christmas day, I awoke early and was grateful for an opportunity to be alone with the Lord for a while before entering into the activities of the day. A little later, we headed down the hill for a children's meeting, the first section of our Christmas service. The old but ever precious Christmas story was told once again in the Shona language by a fellow missionary. Then everyone received a piece of candy. Although it was still early, the heat of the day was upon us, and we decided to move outside under the shade of nearby trees for the next service.

The missionaries indulged in a typical Christmas dinner earlier in the week; but today, Christmas, we ate with our African friends. The menu? *Sadza* (thick corn meal mush), meat with gravy, and tea. Since there were a lot of us to feed, the *sadza* was prepared in an oil drum, cooked outside over an open fire. The tea came from an oil drum, too.

As we were finishing our meal, an ox-drawn cart approached and the stranger asked for directions to the mission hospital. Someone pointed out the doctor in our group, and the oxcart bumped slowly down the hillside toward us. It was crudely made, with wooden wheels, a flat platform, and four poles holding a blanket overhead to provide protection from the blistering African sun.

On the cart lay the patient, a young African woman. She had already been on the way from her home to the hospital for a whole day. Dr. Roland Stephens quickly moved her from the oxcart to his station wagon for the remainder of the journey, about five miles.

Now the day was over. I sat alone on a huge rock formation behind the mission station, drinking in the sweetness of blooming flowers that perfumed the air. The cool breeze was refreshing after the heat of the day. The air was still. The stars were shining – a reminder of that special star which shone almost 2,000 years ago. All the world seemed at peace in the stillness. It was the close of my first Christmas day in Africa.

PHOTO ALBUM

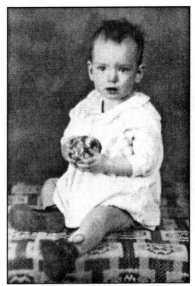

Helen At 16 Months

Helen, CEF Class in Memphis

Studying at Mid South Bible College

*Lorene McIntyre at Bellevue Baptist
Church*

School where Helen taught in Africa

Helen at post office in Africa

Martina, Pirimapun

Helen's House-Pirimapun

Hospital in Pirimapun

Asmat Man

Asmat man with typical headgear

Shirley Rasher at Pirimapun

Helen bathes newborn baby

Village of Senggo

TEAM office with apartment upstairs

View of Manokwari

Shirley Rasher before bookstore

Helen & Bob on honeymoon

Bob and Helen, wedding reception, 1998

Overways with Fraziers, Florida

STRUGGLES

Chapter 20

The missionaries in Rhodesia were a wonderful caring group of people. Relationships developed that made us as close knit as a family. But in my early days — after the initial excitement about finally being on the mission field — I was homesick. I went to the airport to see missionaries off on furlough, and my heart longed to go with them – to return to the familiar, to be with people that I would not see for years to come. I could hardly stand it; I felt so lonely. Although several of us arrived as new missionaries around the same time and were in language study together, the others were married. I was alone. How I longed for someone who understood and with whom I could share my heart, not necessarily a husband – just anyone!

God never causes a needless tear, but He loves us enough to allow struggles and experiences that will help mature us in our walk with Him. The Bible says in Romans 5:3b - 5,

". . . but we glory in tribulations also: knowing that tribulation worketh patience; And patience, experience; and experience, hope: And hope maketh not ashamed; because the love of God is shed abroad in our hearts by the Holy Ghost which is given unto us."

I arose at 5:00 a.m. every morning in order to spend time in language study before going to work in the mission office, but my language progress was discouraging and I felt that the senior missionaries were critical of it. Although the other new missionaries in the language study class could only speak about as well as I, it seemed that they could fall back on the "excuse" of having families, not realizing that being single sometimes seemed to bring on more, varied and time consuming problems than being married. In fact, during those early months, I almost wondered why Paul didn't write the eighth chapter of I Corinthians about the problems of being single – at least on the mission field!

In February, I wrote in my journal,

"The purpose in writing this is not to complain about my fellow missionaries. . . It is to remind me in days ahead to try to be understanding and helpful to those who will follow me as new missionaries . . . With the passing of time, it is possible that I may forget the depths of my own anguish – but I trust that I may not forget the lessons the Lord is teaching me nor lose the compassion

and understanding He would have me gain through these experiences. 2 Corinthians 1:3-4."

I was encouraged in March, 1966, to witness the first two decisions for Christ in the class that I taught in a public school. In my journal, I wrote,

"No opportunity to talk with them afterward, as they had to go to their next class when the bell rang. Only the Lord knows if the decisions were real."

Then a few days later, the next entry read,

"Encouraged in the response of one of the above during today's class. He listened intently and answered many questions."

My primary job was to serve as secretary in the field headquarters office. Discouraged, sometimes I thought, *"Is this all there is? Did I spend all those years in school and preparation for the mission field only to be doing routine office work?"* On one occasion a missionary unknowingly and unintentionally fueled my feelings by commenting that it was a shame I had to be stuck in the office instead of being able to be out in a ministry such as the one in which he was involved in the bush.

Then one day, after I had struggled long enough, God opened my eyes! I realized that I *loved* office work and *loved* sharing in the administration of the field headquarters! I enjoyed the freedom to be creative in taking care of things and realized that I was involved in the work of not just one mission station, but *all* of them! Daily radio contact was maintained with each station. Being centrally located at the mission headquarters gave me the opportunity of becoming acquainted with and closely related to all of the missionaries. I was not limited to one station. I had fallen in love with Rhodesia, the Africans, the missionaries *and* the work! I was ready to put down roots and stay forever, if that was where God wanted me. My feet were becoming firmly rooted in African soil.

Later an American visited the mission station, stopped by the office and asked *"Do you do this all the time or do you do missionary work, too?"* I simply smiled to myself!

In addition to serving as secretary to the Field Chairman, I continued teaching a Bible class each week in a public school. Hospital visitation among women patients in the large government hospital for Africans in the capital city was a regular part of my Sundays. I visited with them, distributed gospel tracts printed in the Shona language and prayed with those who wanted prayer. Then on Sunday afternoons I worked with some other missionaries and African Christians helping to start and develop a Sunday school in an area where there was not one. Sunday evening was a time to worship with a small English speaking Baptist church near the mission headquarters.

Yet the earlier conviction that God had called me to serve in West Irian lingered in my mind. How did it all fit together? I had heard that sometimes God leads in a certain direction, even though He doesn't intend us to ever reach that particular destination, because He has things to accomplish in our lives by so doing. That was wise counsel and is probably true at times. Was it true for me in this case? Had God never actually intended for me to go to West Irian? Had my whole journey in that direction been designed for the purpose of developing me in ways that I could not have been developed otherwise?

In considering the future, I tended more and more to think of living and serving in Rhodesia. I felt that I could be happy staying there. Rhodesia had become home and the missionaries had become family.

But as time passed, I began to realize that the kind of peace which comes from being in the center of God's will was missing from my heart. For many months this was a matter of prayer. What was wrong? Why did I feel as if my prayers were not going any higher than the ceiling? One of the biggest questions facing me was this: Had serving in West Irian been my own desire, or was it really of the Lord? If it was truly of the Lord, how did it fit into my present circumstances?

One morning in November, 1966, as I knelt in despair before the Lord, His voice penetrated the confusion in my heart like a ray of sunshine piercing the darkness, *"No, it is not your desire, Helen."*

I was learning a new lesson: a person can be *in* the Lord's will and *out* of the Lord's will at the same time! *In* His will by being in the place of His choosing for the present, but *out* of His will by accepting as permanent what He intends as temporary.

With this clear answer to months of praying about the matter, I wrote to TEAM headquarters in the USA and also shared my thoughts with the Rhodesia Field Chairman and Field Council. Since it was likely that months or years of waiting still remained before God would move me to West Irian, it seemed best not to publicize the matter until something definite developed.

From the home office, Dr. Kuehl responded by saying that the latest missionaries applying to West Irian for visas had been rejected. However, my name would be placed on the list to reapply when my turn came.

Another year rolled by. I continued in the work in Rhodesia, now rising at 4:30 a.m. to study the Shona language before going to the office and also attending Shona language classes at the University in the evenings. On January 16, 1968, I completed the final part of the field's Shona language requirements when I passed the oral examination. Though I knew it would take many years of practice for me to become really fluent, I was feeling more comfortable with the language.

A little less than two months later, on March 11, 1968, the visa application forms for West Irian arrived and I began gathering the necessary documents: medical reports, police certificates, passport photos and an x-ray, etc. The last item needed for the visa application reached me on Monday, April 1, 1968, and the following day all was sent by registered mail to the Mission headquarters in the USA.

April 15 - 21, 1968, the annual field conference was held on our mission station at Hatfield. It was good to have our General Director, Dr. Vernon Mortenson, and his wife Frances with us from the USA and also Dick Winchell from TEAM South Africa. Dick and Marge Winchell were being transferred to the home office in Wheaton, IL.

Conference days were full, but one evening Dr. Mortenson and I had an opportunity to talk privately in the field office. My heart was made heavy by what he had to say when I learned that he felt it necessary to discourage my going to West Irian. His reason seemed a good one — my health. This was not because of any particular problem, as my health had actually improved during the time in Rhodesia. But apparently questions lingered in the minds of some as to whether I was physically strong enough to survive in the jungles of New Guinea.

After praying more about it, I felt no peace of heart about withdrawing the visa application. Neither did I feel it was right to go against the advice of the General Director. He asked, *"What will you do if I just tell you that you can't go to West Irian?"* With all the respect I could muster in answering the person with ultimate authority, my sincere response was, *"I feel that I must be submissive to those who are over me in the Lord, but I believe He is going to move you to let me go!"*

We came to an agreement that I would return to the USA for further medical examinations and also to consult with Dr. Ken Dresser, TEAM's missionary doctor from West Irian, while he was on furlough.

Dr. Mortenson and I both seemed comfortable with this agreement. If medical clearance was granted, I would work in the home office of the mission until the visa came. Dr. Mortenson advised me that it would probably be another two years before a visa for West Irian could be obtained, if one was granted.

My departure from Africa was scheduled for September 1968.

VISA!

Chapter 21

O n May 4, 1968, a letter from Lorene brought the good news that she was engaged to be married to a young man by the name of Bill Overway! They were making tentative plans for an August wedding and asked if it would be possible for me to return to the USA in August instead of September so that I could be Lorene's maid of honor.

Though Lorene had been accepted for missionary service with TEAM when we attended candidate school together in 1961, it had not worked out for her to go overseas. Strangely, humanly speaking, she was the one who eventually could not obtain medical clearance. Lorene had been a farm girl and a hard worker with all the appearances of vibrant health during our college days. People always seemed to question whether or not I would be able to go to a foreign mission field, but never whether Lorene would! However, even in those days she had the beginnings of orthopedic problems that increased in intensity and required multiple surgeries over the years. Later in life she developed severe arthritic problems and other disabilities. While I was in Africa, Lorene accepted an invitation to serve at TEAM headquarters and moved to Wheaton, IL, where the mission's international headquarters was now located. They built new offices and moved from Chicago after I left for Africa. It was in Illinois that William Overway, who was employed at the Moody Bible Institute in Chicago, came into her life!

Return to the USA in August? For such an important event, perhaps leaving Africa a month earlier than planned could be worked out. However, a few days later, my world was turned upside down once more! A letter from Dr. Mortenson arrived, suggesting that I wait for another year before returning to the States and plan to return in September of 1969, rather than September 1968. Then it was recommended that I wait until 1970 before returning to the USA, as no more visa applications for West Irian would be processed until after the plebiscite in West Irian during the summer of 1969.

Just when things seemed blackest, a letter came from West Irian informing me that this news had been a mistake! Whether that meant my visa application was being processed or not, I wasn't sure.

On August 11, 1968, once again I poured out my heart in my journal.

> *"How good it is to be in the hands of an omnipotent Father. Without any insistence on my part – just sharing what I felt to be His*

leading and why – and after further prayer and waiting on Him, all involved have concurred with the step of my return to the States in September (of this year). Present plans point to a September 20 departure."

Lorene and Bill's wedding was moved up to June. I could not be there in person, but my thoughts and prayers were there and my heart rejoiced with theirs.

On September 20, 1968, an aircraft ascended from the Salisbury Airport taking me with it and leaving my world behind. I did not want to leave Africa, but my heart knew that I was taking the right step in obedience to God's leading. When we crossed the river dividing Rhodesia from South Africa, I could not keep back the tears, and when the plane landed in New York and it was time to disembark, I wanted to get back on it and return with it to Africa.

Of course, there were positive aspects of returning to the USA. It was wonderful to visit with family and friends and to revisit familiar places. I enjoyed visiting TEAM's beautiful new facilities in Wheaton, IL, for the first time. Then after some other travel, I returned and began working in the office on Monday, October 14, 1968. My heart was torn between two worlds — Africa and America.

The following year brought a variety of experiences, including the enjoyable job at TEAM headquarters and lots of travel. A wonderful apartment mate by the name of Jennifer Berry helped assuage my loneliness for Africa, since she was a South

African by birth. We tromped through the snow on wintry days, entertained friends in our cozy apartment, and shared our hearts and aspirations — as well as our problems and burdens. Jenny was a missionary nurse with TEAM and on July 12, 1969, she departed from Chicago's O'Hare International Airport to serve at the mission hospital in Zululand, South Africa.

A very important trip took place for me that year in February, 1969, when I went to Toronto, Ontario, Canada, to visit with Dr. and Mrs. Kenneth Dresser regarding medical clearance for West Irian. Not only did Dr. Dresser give his approval, but he and his wife Sylvia advised the mission that they would like for me to work on the same mission station with them! In April, 1969, Dr. Andrew Karsgaard, TEAM's Medical Director, also granted his approval. Were the doors to West Irian beginning to swing open?

May 1969 found me in Portland, Oregon, for TEAM's Annual Conference. In June, it was perhaps a bit difficult to find me anywhere! The odometer on the small car that I rented from TEAM registered over 5,000 miles between Wheaton, Ohio, Kentucky, Tennessee, Mexico, Louisiana, Arkansas, Tennessee again, southern Illinois and back to Wheaton!

Then came the big day! October 24, 1969, was a date to go down in history – well, at least in *my* history! A little more than a year had passed since my departure from Rhodesia. I was at work in the TEAM office when Goldye Gustafson, the General Director's secretary, phoned and asked me to come to Dr. Mortenson's office. As I entered his office he greeted me, smiled and handed me a cable from

Indonesia. It read simply, *"Edds visa granted!"* I wept, and I think that there were a few tears in that office besides mine.

WEST IRIAN

Chapter 22

Sunday night, March 1, 1970, shortly before 10:00 p.m. I found myself aboard a large Japan Airlines jet at the Los Angeles International Airport, fastening my seat belt and preparing for takeoff. Packing, paper work and inoculations were behind me, and my goodbyes had been said. My journey across the Pacific Ocean was about to begin. Almost nine years after my appointment to West Irian in July of 1961, I was on the way.

I couldn't quite fathom that I was about to begin a journey which would take me halfway around the world! It simply seemed natural and right: the next step in the progressive will of God for my life.

The "Wall Street Journal" had recently written of West Irian in their publication dated August 12, 1969, as follows.

> *"West Irian is the western half of the giant South pacific island of New Guinea. It's the size of France with an estimated 800,000*

inhabitants . . . divided into some 150 distinct tribes speaking as many mutually unintelligible languages . . . a vast, remote, primitive territory, large parts of which are still literally in the Stone Age . . . The extent to which West Irian remains an unexplored wilderness is staggering, all the more so at a time when man's frontier has extended to the moon. There are rivers here wider than the Mississippi, but whose muddy waters have never been parted by a boat's prow. The 30-foot crocodiles that infest them have never had to fear a hunter. There are mountain valleys so remote and mist-shrouded that they have never been surveyed even by plane . . . There are several hundred thousand natives whose only links with civilization are the tiny missionary stations that dot the interior . . . The missions' small fleets of single-engine Cessnas are the only transportation system throughout most of the territory."

Opening my small New Testament, I asked, *"Father what would be a good verse with which to begin this journey?"* My eyes fell on Ephesians 6:16, *"Above all, taking the shield of faith, wherewith ye shall be able to quench all the fiery darts of the wicked."* I decided that might be quite appropriate. As things turned out, it was!

Traveling as directly as possible toward my destination, I stopped only where required: Honolulu, Tokyo, Hong Kong, Bangkok, Singapore, Jakarta,

Makassar, and Biak, eventually reaching Sentani which is located near Jayapura, the capital city of West Irian.

It was customary for West Irian bound missionaries to stop in Jakarta (capital of Indonesia) on the island of Java for clearance, even though a visa was in hand. My clearance in Jakarta went through quickly. I arrived there on Tuesday night, March 3, 1970, and was cleared on Friday morning, March 6. The couple of days in Jakarta provided an opportunity for a small beginning in learning the Indonesian language. Before leaving Jakarta, my vocabulary consisted of a few practical phrases such as "*Terima kasih*" ("Thank You") and *Ma'af* ("Excuse me")!

Those days also provided an opportunity to begin learning their customs with the help of an Indonesian girl who spoke English and invited me to her home. As was true in Africa, she advised me that it was rude to use my left hand either to receive anything or to hand something to someone.

Another lesson is comical in retrospect, but was embarrassing at the time of learning! It was related to table manners. A drink, something that tasted similar to weak Kool Aid, was served. Determined to be a good guest and a good missionary, I drank it down to the last drop. Immediately my glass was refilled. I am not sure how long this continued, perhaps until they ran out of the beverage. It was only later that I learned it is not polite to drink all of a beverage (that was an indication to the hostess that I wanted more) or to eat every bite of food on one's plate!

With these beginning lessons in language and

culture in place, I boarded one of the twice-weekly flights to Biak on Saturday, March 7, reaching Biak by mid-afternoon the same day. Biak is a small island located on the equator, my first point of entry into West Irian. It was not my final destination, however, and I had no intention of spending time there. But as things turned out, it became my final stop for that day.

For some reason, I was bumped from the continuing flight to Sentani. There I was "in the middle of nowhere," not knowing what to do and not yet able to speak the language! But God was with me and had two more of His "angels" ready. Mike Hannas and his wife Mae (missionaries in Biak with another mission) invited me into their home. In fact, Mike had come to the airport to meet the incoming plane just in case there was a missionary on board. Once again official clearance was required and Mike helped me obtain this. It was granted three days later on Tuesday, March 10. But as there was no onward flight available until Friday, it was necessary for me to remain on the island of Biak until then.

On Friday, March 13, 1970, the plane from Biak landed at the Sentani Airport about 11:00 a.m., and I finally set foot on the mainland of West Irian for the first time. No one was at the small airport to meet me and my Indonesian vocabulary of "*excuse me*" and "*thank you*" didn't go very far in communicating my needs to anyone! Apparently no one there spoke English.

Once again, God sent an "angel" in the form of a fellow passenger — a Pakistani man who spoke

English. He came to my aid and helped me figure out what to do. The road to the Missionary Aviation Fellowship station was pointed out to me, and so – leaving my luggage at the airport — I set out on foot in that direction. Before I got all the way there, an Irianese man saw me walking along the dusty road and hurried to the mission station exclaiming, *"There's a white woman walking along the air strip!"* An MAF missionary quickly hopped into a jeep and drove down to pick me up. I later learned that the missionaries had previously met four planes, looking for me. So they *had* tried!

That was my welcome to West Irian. What in the world would happen next?

My next destination was Amar, a small village on the south coast of West Irian. Plans to travel there on March 18 were changed by the weather, a not infrequent happening in West Irian. But on Thursday, March 19, 1970, at last I was in the air, traveling in a float plane which would land on the river at the small south coast village of Amar.

As we flew over the expanse of jungle, pilot Bob Breuker cheerfully quipped, *"Don't worry about the fact that we have no wheels. If we go down, it won't matter whether or not we have wheels!"*

On Sunday, I wrote to friends back home from Amar:

> *"Was it only a month ago tomorrow that I said goodbye and took wings from O'Hare Airport? Seems more like a year of experiences since then! It was good to reach my destination after being on the way nineteen*

days and to be able to unpack and settle down for a while, as of last Thursday . . . The scenery between here and Sentani (about three hours by air in a Cessna aircraft) is breathtakingly beautiful, especially the mountains. We passed so close to the mountain peaks in one place that I felt I could almost touch them if I stuck my hand out the window! Glad I had a good pilot! We came by float plane and landed on the river here at Amar."

"Amar is a picturesque little village with two rows of thatch-roofed houses, built on stilts, facing each other. It is bordered by tall coconut palms and surrounded by the jungle, the river and the ocean."

Two single ladies staffed the Amar mission station and worked with the Mimika tribe. Margery Smith was from California and Margaret Stringer was from South Carolina. We met for the first time on the river bank at Amar. I was there to study the Indonesian language, and Margaret was to be my instructor.

Marge and Margaret shared a house at the end of the village. They had fixed it up so that it was quite attractive, though of course not elaborate. It was built on stilts and had a metal roof and wood floors. The inside walls were of varnished palm wood strips. There was piped-in rain water and a bathroom, but no electricity. Kerosene was used for cooking and for lights.

Some of the lessons I learned at Amar included these: 1) it was best not to ask what I was eating when eating with the villagers. After all, a lot of our hangups are only psychological. 2) it is possible to hold one's breath and swallow food at the same time, especially when the food has an objectionable odor. These lessons were afforded me by my first potluck dinner with the villagers on Easter Sunday, March 29, 1970, just ten days after my arrival.

A few days after my arrival, it was necessary for Margaret to leave the mission station for several days. She turned over the clinic to me while she was away. My "vast knowledge" of the Indonesian language now included such words as *sakit* (sick / hurt) and *minum* (drink / swallow). Thus I was able to learn where the patient was hurting or having a problem, and also to give medicine and instructions to drink or swallow it. Marge, of course, helped me with the interpretation of more complex conversations. Perhaps the biggest challenge was a boy with a fish hook stuck through his thumb, which by God's grace I was able to remove. Another memorable patient was a sweet lady who was suffering from tuberculosis, a prevalent disease. The tribal people often had tuberculosis of the bones, and in her case there was an abscess in the spinal area which required cleansing and dressing each day, plus daily injections of medication.

In addition to flying in a plane with no wheels, travel in a dugout canoe was a new and exciting experience! Around mid April, Margaret and I traveled with some Irianese people in a canoe that was equipped with a motor. What a surprise when, as we whizzed along, a huge fish jumped out of the ocean and smacked me in the face! Then, sailing over my shoulder it crashed through the sun umbrella that I was holding, hit someone behind me and flopped back out into the ocean! Fortunately, it didn't break my glasses. Unfortunately, we didn't get to eat it for supper.

Margaret said that I was beginning to speak Indonesian with a Mimika accent, and she felt it would be wise to move to another location for language study.

Thus it was decided that Margaret and I would move to Kokanao, a small town on the south coast of West Irian. Kokanao was not far from Amar, but there was no road between the two. We traveled by boat or missionary aircraft. In Kokanao there was a little store or two, an airstrip and a government post. TEAM missionaries had served there in past years and their Kingstrand (prefab metal) house was still usable and provided a place for us to live. On April 28, 1970, we made the move.

First of all, we set about cleaning the little house and making it livable. It had three small bedrooms, a living room, a combination kitchen/dining area and a front porch. There was also a bathroom behind the house. My bedroom furniture consisted of a single bed and a TV tray which became a bedside table. My suitcase served as a dresser, along with a basket and a cardboard box. There were two shelves with a wire strung underneath them to serve as a closet. Sweeping the floors was easy, as the dirt slipped right through the cracks between the planks of the floor.

On April 30, two other new missionaries, Bill and Laura Fay who were with the Unevangelized Fields Mission, came to Kokanao to join the language study sessions.

MAF planes were scheduled to come every three weeks, bringing our mail, a little fresh meat (there was not room to store much of it in the small freezer compartment of the kerosene refrigerator), some eggs and also some fresh vegetables that were grown at the mountain stations. The south coast was basically a swamp and not favorable to vegetable gardens. A green plant called *konkone* grew wild in some of the ditches and it could be cooked and eaten as a green vegetable. We took turns with planning and cooking meals, and I began to learn that there must be a thousand ways to cook canned corn beef!

In order to help us learn the language without a particular accent, we were provided with five Indonesian speaking men who served as informants. They helped us with pronunciation, intonations and other aspects of the Indonesian language.

Margaret and Marge had one short-wave radio between them, and since Marge would be staying alone at Amar until Margaret returned in several months we felt that we should leave it with her. So, for a while, Margaret and I lost touch with the outside world except for the mail delivery by the MAF plane every three weeks and the two-way radio communication with other mission stations. That was available during the daytime, but we could not count on that connection at night. We remarked that the world could be in World War III and we wouldn't even know about it! But we immersed ourselves in Indonesian language study. No one around us spoke English.

I finished the last lap of initial language study on my first birthday in West Irian, September 25, 1970. That evening Margaret combined a graduation party with a birthday party for me. Our refreshments were homemade donuts and Milo (a chocolate drink made with powdered milk), and we sang hymns, and had a time of fellowship.

Now it was time to move on to Pirimapun, where I had been assigned to serve at the small mission hospital. Pirimapun was also on the south coast of West Irian, but a long way from both Amar and Kokanao. The Mimika people of Amar tried to discourage me from going to Pirimapun, informing me that the Asmat people were cannibals and would kill and eat me!

PIRIMAPUN

Chapter 23

On September 30, 1970, I departed from Kokanao and headed for Pirimapun aboard an MAF cessna aircraft. En route we stopped at Yaosakor, another south coast village where TEAM had a ministry among the Asmat tribe. Yaosakor was also the south coast base of the Missionary Aviation Fellowship.

The Dressers were not at Pirimapun at that time, as Dr. Ken Dresser and two of their sons had hepatitis. They were being cared for at the hospital station of another mission, which was located in the mountains. It appeared that I would be alone at Pirimapun temporarily, but that was okay with me. I looked forward to getting to my own home and getting settled. God would be with me and I figured that with six months of Indonesian language study under my belt, I could communicate well enough to get by until the Dressers returned.

However, leaving me alone at Pirimapun was not

okay with MAF's south coast pilot Bob Breuker! In fact, he refused to take me and leave me there alone, when I had never been there before and suggested that Margaret accompany me. Margaret had previously offered to go with me, but I felt that she needed to return to her own work at Amar and encouraged her to do that. Nevertheless, since I was not allowed to proceed alone, I finally accepted Margaret's offer and she flew with me. We spent the night at Yaosakor and then flew on to Pirimapun the next day.

The Asmat village of Pirimapun lay alongside the sparkling waters of the Arafura Sea in the Cook's Bay area of the south coast of West Irian. Several years earlier, in answer to prayer for help with the medical needs in West Irian, Dr. Ken Dresser and his wife Sylvia, an RN, answered the call to serve there. Missionaries Bob Frazier and Elmer Schmidt met Dr. Dresser and took him to the Asmat region for an extensive survey, as they considered where to build a mission hospital. Later, Bob wrote,

> *"People of the Cook's Bay area were among the fiercest and most primitive I had ever seen. The doctor had to be careful for his family. At times he and his wife, Sylvia, were threatened. Fortunately, the government had set up a post there. Thus they had some protection."*

According to history, Captain James Cook at one time visited that area in his search for new lands.

Some of his men went ashore to explore but never returned.

By the time I arrived at Pirimapun a small hospital had been built by TEAM. The landscape was dotted by the small government post and a government-operated elementary school with a dirt floor and thatched roof, in addition to the hospital, and an unpaved airstrip ran parallel with the beach. There were two missionary dwellings. The Dressers lived in one of them. The other, previously used by missionaries who were forced to return to the States by serious health problems, was designated for me. The Asmat people lived in houses built on stilts high above the mud, and pigs jostled along beneath their houses.

Pirimapun's only "street" was a dirt road which ran alongside my house, extending from the river on one end to the jungle and sea at the other end of the village, all within easy walking distance. The river curved so that it flowed behind my house, separating my back yard from dense jungle.

Pirimapun was isolated, but life there was far from dull! On Tuesday mornings, the hospital's baby clinic bustled with activity as mothers in grass skirts brought naked babies to be weighed, have a bath, be given vitamins and checked over in general. A bath as we know it was something new to them, and usually the little faces were caked with dirt. Mothers were shown how to use soap and to bathe the babies. The color of the bath water afterward was rewarding, giving evidence of a worthwhile effort! Serious health problems were referred to the doctor and malnutrition cases were started on supplementary feedings.

On Friday mornings, the mother-baby clinic experienced activity again, though not as noisy as Tuesday's. Friday was when the mothers to be came in for a checkup. Later, when their babies were born, they could either come to us at the hospital or call us to come to them in the village.

Every day except Sunday the hospital clinic was open to those who had any sort of physical problem (and, of course, medical help was available on Sundays, too, when needed). A worship service was held each morning on the front porch of the hospital and following that the hospital opened for business.

Most of the medical work was done on an out-patient basis. However, for serious illnesses which required hospitalization, there was an in-patient ward behind the hospital. It was built of native materials, on stilts, with a thatched roof. Like the patients' own homes, it had no beds and they slept on the floor or on grass mats. Scattered throughout the ward were places where fires could be built, again like those in their own homes. These provided the family with a place to cook meals and eat with the patient, and the smoke helped reduce the number of mosquitos.

On November 12, 1970, Martina, the chief's daughter, came to visit me. Although I could not speak Asmat, the local language, she spoke Indonesian and so we were able to communicate in that way. There were two reasons why I had invited her to come. One was to offer her a job helping me in various ways. The other, and perhaps the more important reason, was to begin establishing a friendship with her and ultimately with other girls and women in the village. Martina was an intelligent and pleasant young woman, and eventually she was trained to help me not only around the house but also in the hospital.

I made it a practice to sit down with her every morning for a break and a devotional time together, using the Indonesian Bible. Our first Bible story was from the Old Testament, where Moses lifted up the serpent and those who looked at it were saved from death. Then we turned to the story in the New Testament, where the Lord Jesus Christ used that story to illustrate that He would be lifted up on a cross, thereby guaranteeing that if we look to Him and trust Him, we will be saved from spiritual death. Martina and I developed a deep friendship, and I was destined to share a crisis in her life in the year that followed.

Along with other activities, ongoing language requirements included a required number of hours of language study each week. We were also asked to read a prescribed number of pages in the Indonesian language in a book or periodical. This was in preparation for taking each succeeding language examination and moving on to another level of study. Some interesting books in the Indonesian language were available and since I enjoy reading, that part of the assignment was the most welcome. The problem was finding time and energy to do it!

I loved the tranquil greenness of the jungle, the quiet beauty of the water and the thrill of God's handiwork in the sunsets. Neither the river nor the sea were places to swim, however, as there were poisonous snakes and stinging fish in the sea and crocodiles in the river.

My first Christmas in West Irian was approaching and Marge Smith and Margaret Stringer accepted an invitation to spend it with me at Pirimapun. Margaret arrived on Christmas Eve; Marge had come several days earlier. Combining our supplies, including a turkey imported from Australia, we all enjoyed a delicious Christmas dinner together with the Dresser family.

We did not know it then, but a few days later we would share in a lot more excitement than any of us had anticipated during this holiday season! In the wee hours of the morning of December 30, 1970, our lives and future plans for the work at Pirimapun were changed forever.

Experiencing the effects of a typhoon at sea, the water came rushing over the airstrip, rendering it permanently unusable as an airstrip and changing it into a sandy beach of sea shells, logs and other debris. During the night I awoke to the sound of huge logs battering my house as the waves roughly pushed them forward. Still lying in bed, I felt the spray of salt water on my face in the darkness, as the water splashed up between the wooden floor boards.

Daylight revealed a coating of mud inside the house. Part of that day was spent cleaning mud off the wood floors, only to have a repeat performance the following night! Large wooden poles were erected around the house to protect it from further battering by the logs as they washed ashore with the tide. Ken came over and put my kerosene refrigerator up on blocks to protect the kerosene container and the wick below the refrigerator from getting water in them. The Dressers' house, a little higher off the ground, was not flooded.

As the water entered my house, it brought with it little creatures that swam around in the bathroom. Eventually the flood water turned to mere dampness and a multiplied number of centipedes, especially in the bathroom, were the only residual problem.

The next extremely high tide was anticipated the following December, and so it appeared that a move before that time was imperative. Where, when and how would be considered by the annual field conference in June. Moving a hospital, even a small one, plus homes and other buildings would be no small task, especially in a place where roads and trucks were nonexistent!

In the meantime, life and ministry at Pirimapun must be maintained. My bond with the Asmat people was growing, and it would be difficult to say goodbye. I had come to feel at home sitting on the floor of smoke filled huts in the little village of Pirimapun. The people showed skulls of deceased loved ones to me and I learned that, as we keep photographs, they sometimes kept a skull. I sat with them when someone died, and sometimes delivered medicine in the village to those who were ill and unable to come to the hospital.

Since it appeared that we would most likely move into an area where another tribal language was used, there was no need for me to continue Asmat language lessons. Instead, I concentrated on learning and improving my use of the national language, Indonesian. Some of the Asmat people could speak Indonesian.

On September 30, 1971, I wrote to friends in the USA,

> *"Did you know that white people have tough skin? Last night after prayer meeting, we were sitting around talking and they got to talking about cannibalistic practices. It's a wonder I slept so well after that! Two of the men there evidently have eaten people in their pre-Christian days. Some of the practices are more horrible than I had thought. I thought they just ate them, but they said that sometimes they have a party and tie up the captive and cut slices off him while he's still alive and cook the meat and eat it. They said it's torture and I can believe it! They talked about roasting little children, and I learned a bit about how they sever the heads of captives and take out the brain, etc. There are several spots to aim at if you want to kill a person, and you would think the guy had a course in anatomy as he was so accurate in pointing out where to stab or shoot (with spear or arrow) the heart, the spinal column at the lower part of the back, the temple, the eye, etc. I asked one of the fellows why they ate people. He said, 'Well, it's because they don't know the Lord, and they just enjoy it.' He said that sometimes too it is just because they are*

hungry and it is easier to go and kill a human being than to hunt a wild pig and kill it!! He's the one who told me that white people have tough skin. I said, 'You mean we're not as tasty?' I guess he thought I was insulted, as he quickly replied, 'Oh, no, it's not that you don't taste good; it's just the skin that's tough. It's like the skin of a pig!' Actually, I wasn't insulted at all – I was rather pleased with the idea that I might not be too appetizing! And if I keep my weight down, maybe I'll be even less appealing! As we left to go home, I heard someone walking away in the other direction whistling the hymn, "Love Found a Way," and it brought a real thrill to my heart to think of the words to that hymn and to realize how very true they are.

Wonderful love that rescued me,
Sunk deep in sin,
Guilty and vile as I could be –
No hope within;
When every ray of light had fled,
O glorious day!
Raising my soul from out the dead,
Love found a way.

Love bro't my Saviour here to die
On Calvary
For such a sinful wretch as I–
How can it be?
Love bridged the gulf

Twixt me and heav'n,
Taught me to pray;
I am redeemed, set free, forgiv'n–
Love found a way.

Chorus:

Love found a way
To redeem my soul,
Love found a way
That could make me whole;
Love sent my Lord
To the cross of shame,
Love found a way–
O praise His holy name!

MARTINA

Chapter 24

This is Martina's story, a day I was blessed to share.

June 17, 1971

Today was my wedding day. But its dawning brought only feelings of repulsion mixed with terror! I had fought against it. I had suffered beatings in attempts to force me into submission. More than once I had fled from the village.

But now, today, my father said that I must go through with it! This is our way of life. If one's father insists, there remains no avenue of escape. My marriage is not mine alone; it affects others because it is our custom to function on an exchange basis. That is, a girl from one family is given in exchange for a girl from another family. My refusal was holding up another wedding as well as my own.

I thought of the man to whom I was promised and a chill crept over my being. If only I could at least respect him as a decent person. But only one description came to my mind: no good. He is reputed to be a thief. Besides that, I am in love with another man and he with me, but we are not free to choose each other.

Panic forced me to act quickly. Once more I must make an attempt to escape, or at least to delay this horrible thing a little longer! Without taking time to dress, I ran from the house. My bare feet flew swiftly down the round branch-steps of our hut, which is built on stilts, and onto the rough wooden walkway that runs in front of the row of houses, then to the soft earth with its gravel-like carpet of broken seashells.

Where could I go? The only possible place of even temporary refuge which presented itself to my confused mind was the nearby home of the missionary with whom I work.

Embarrassed to be there without my clothes (usually I wear a cotton skirt and blouse when I am at her house), I stopped by her bathroom, just off the back porch, and wrapped a towel around my body. Then, opening the kitchen door, I slipped quietly inside. Nona Helen ("Nona" is an Indonesian word meaning an unmarried lady) was sitting in the living room, reading her Bible. It was just after 6:00 a.m. and she was surprised to see me so early. I myself had not known the day before that today was to be my wedding day and so she didn't know either. She assumed that I had merely come unusually early and simply said, "Selamat pagi" ("good morning"). I went into her bedroom, sat down on the bed, and awaited the inevitable.

The inevitable was not long in catching up with me. From the bedroom, I heard Nona answer the door and then heard my brother's voice asking if I was there. He told her that I was to be married today, I had run away, and when my father came she must hand me over to him.

After he had gone, she came into the bedroom where I sat motionless, wrapped in my rose-pink towel, and looked at me. Heart-perplexed in an awareness of her powerlessness to stop what was happening, a silent cry for help ascended heavenward. "Dear God, please show me what to do," she prayed.

When my father arrived a few minutes later, Nona asked permission for me to stay long enough to have a bath, which I normally take daily at her house. She said that a girl should especially be allowed a bath on her wedding day. "Anything to stall for time," she thought. Father agreed and went away for a while. The clean, warm water with its soapy fragrance was refreshing on an ordinary day. Today, its warmth could hardly touch the icy fingers of fear and dread that were clutching at my heart.

While I was bathing and dressing in a cotton hospital uniform, Nona was consulting our missionary doctor, Ken Dresser. Then she returned to the house and prepared a simple breakfast for the two of us. We prayed together and asked God to undertake and have His will.

We were eating when my father again appeared at the door. Apparently the doctor's pleas had fallen on deaf ears. Father wanted to take me with him and get on with the details of the marriage. There were things to be counted out and exchanged between the families: possibly axes, clothing or whatever other treasures might have been stored away for such an occasion.

Nona's heart was aching and she was praying for a miracle. Outwardly she smiled and asked my father if he could take the time to come in and join us for a cup of coffee. He sat down at the table while she poured a cup of steaming hot coffee from the percolator and set before him a piece of coffee cake.

I had been learning a little about cooking and, as it happened, this very coffee cake was one of the things we had made together. She mentioned this to my father, who was looking around the little house with obvious approval of its modest furnishings. He eyed the little two-burner kerosene cookstove with the small portable oven sitting on one of the burners. What a marvel in comparison with the fire on the floor of our hut!

Nona mentioned that I was learning many things. The faint hope that lightened my understanding was evident in my eyes as our glances met momentarily. I realized that she was presenting an argument to my father, without putting it into words: if he forced me into a marriage such as was planned for today, I would be giving up all that I was learning and enter a life of nothing but hard work and servitude to a man I did not and could not love. On the other hand, if I were allowed to continue working and learning, it would not only be a wonderful opportunity for me but would also provide a sort of prestige for my father.

Both Nona and I were hanging onto every shred of hope. I said nothing. My father and Nona talked on, but the subject of my wedding did not once enter verbally into the conversation.

About half an hour and more coffee later, Father rose and said that we must be going. My hope plummeted and so did Nona's. She knew she could not change my father's mind by arguing, nor could she possibly protect me forcibly. She simply asked, "This man you want your daughter to marry today, is he a good man?" and then added, "We prayed about it before you came and asked for God's will to be done."

As he prepared to leave, my father did a strange thing. He invited Nona to come with us to our home for the wedding arrangements! She agreed. This was not an agreement to the marriage, but rather a matter of staying with me as long as possible.

When we arrived at the village a few minutes later, a clean grass mat was spread on the floor of our hut for Nona and me. We sat on the mat for a while, waiting for things to progress. I was sick with dread. Then some of the married women came over to me, carrying a garment worn only by a married Asmat woman (a bikini-like brief made of grass). The fatal hour had arrived!

Resisting their endeavors, I refused to take off the cotton hospital uniform and don the wedding garment. Another woman joined their forces and they tried harder to get it on me forcibly. By now I was crying, and Nona, still sitting beside me with face buried in one hand, was also sobbing quietly. Her heart ached with what mine was going through and with a knowledge of what the moments and years beyond this hour would hold. A sixteen-year old girl, intelligent, already with some schooling and understanding of how the world outside our little jungle village lives, forced into marriage with a man she not only disliked, but despised, and pushed into a life of nothing much but cutting and carrying wood, fishing for food, sitting in the village, hard work. I can read, but most likely there would never again be anything to read. Although our Asmat language is still in the process of being analyzed and is as yet unwritten, I can speak and read Indonesian, the national language.

No one could help me now but God, and even He would need to work a miracle if I were to be spared at this point!

My brother went over to Nona and asked her to leave, as it appeared that they were going to have to beat me into submission. "I'm going with you!" I cried, but as I jumped up to follow her, I was forcibly restrained.

Nona wept as she walked home. One of the Asmat men who passed her as he headed toward the village said, "Don't cry, Nona, it's just our way." Moments later in her own home, only a short distance from mine, she fell down on her knees beside the bed with a heavy and broken heart, weeping as she prayed for me. "Dear God," she pleaded, "only a miracle can save her, but <u>You</u> can still perform that miracle."

Suddenly the unbelievable happened! My father, the village chief, violated the traditional marriage arrangements that have bound our women as far back as anyone can remember! Sending away the man I despised, he sent for the man I loved! In little more than a few minutes, the bridegrooms had been exchanged and I found myself being wed to the man of my choice!

It was a miracle! My nightmare wedding had turned into a dream fulfilled, a prayer abundantly answered. In the afternoon, we were married in the church in addition to our village wedding this morning. My husband agrees to my continuing to work and learn with Nona.

As we approached the village, walking home from the church after our miraculous wedding, my heart was filled to overflowing. But suddenly screams rent the air, the cry of another girl being forced into a marriage she did not want. It is a familiar sound.

One by one, God is changing my people. Nona was yet to have another unforgettable experience of seeing God at work among us before she had to move away from our village.

YAKOB

Chapter 25

L ife at Pirimapun continued, filled to the brim. In addition to medical work with the local people, we also provided medical care for missionaries and often needed space to accommodate them. They came to Pirimapun to be seen by Dr. Dresser regarding health problems or to deliver babies and usually stayed with me. The Dressers had three children with them (five when the two oldest were home for school holidays). The room that I normally used for a pantry was turned into a delivery room when missionaries came to give birth.

A house previously occupied by a national worker was now empty, and we decided that I would move into it and turn what had been my house into a guest house for missionaries.

My new home was smaller, but quite cozy and adequate, and I really liked it. It was closer to the village and I liked that, too. Living there brought new and interesting experiences.

A little bathroom was attached to the house, just past a small back porch. The house was wooden with a metal roof, but the bathroom walls were made of *gaba-gaba* (the large stems from leaves of sago palm trees; these "stems" were thick, several feet long, and averaged from one to three inches in width) and had a thatched roof. It boasted a commode and a shower. The shower was a galvanized bucket with a shower head in the bottom. There was no running water in the bathroom, but the shower bucket was easily filled with piped-in rainwater carried from the kitchen, which I heated on the small kerosene cook stove. During a shower, the water simply flowed from the bucket through the floor to the ground below. If *gaba-gaba* could talk, those bathroom walls could relate a few funny stories of their own!

The village people were not embarrassed to stand at windows and peer into a house. As the occupant moved from room to room, the group of villagers often followed their movements by going to the next window. Although it took a little adjusting, eventually I realized that this had its perks. Since they unabashedly watched me and whatever I was doing, I could feel free to do the same thing in their homes in the village! They wanted to know how these foreigners lived and they also welcomed me to see how they lived, to sit around the fire on the floor of their huts, ask questions and just be with them. They showed me the skulls they kept in the house and told me about the deceased loved ones these represented. One day when I was sitting there visiting, one of the men sat down and began to put a bone through his nose. He looked at me and said, *"Don't worry, Nona, I'm just getting ready for a party!"*

One day I traveled with them by canoe into the jungle and watched them glean *sago*, their staple food. Although I had never cared much for *sago*, the taste and consistency of which to me was like a cross between a rubber band and soft plastic, I appreciated it much more after seeing the hard work involved in obtaining it. It was made from the pulp of a sago palm tree. After choosing the tree, chopping it down, opening and pulverizing the inside of the trunk, the pulp was mixed with water from the swamp and squeezed. The pulp was then thrown away and the liquid was caught and allowed to harden into a chalk-like substance. Later, this substance would be pulverized or grated, wrapped in banana leaves – or packed into a small flat tin can, if they had obtained one that a missionary had discarded – and cooked over an open fire.

But back to the talking bathroom walls! The bathroom was one place where viewers from the outside were not allowed. However, one day after taking a shower, I turned around and there – peering through a small space in the *gaba-gaba* walls – was the beautiful brown eye of a chocolate-skinned boy. He seemed as startled as I when I saw him and quickly disappeared. I thought, *"Well, I guess now he knows I'm white all over!"*

One of the challenges of that bathroom was that the roof leaked directly over the commode! Why it couldn't have chosen to leak over the shower instead,

I have no idea; that could have saved hauling water! But perhaps it wouldn't have given me the humorous memories provided by the big leak over the toilet! The funniest was when I was sitting on the commode one night during a tropical rain. It was necessary to hold an umbrella while sitting there when it was raining. That was not such a big deal. However, one night, it was not only raining but was also quite dark. There I sat, with an umbrella in one hand and a lamp in the other, wondering how to manage anything else!

Another night, a big frog decided to join me for my bucket shower. I had just finished showering and was holding my only light, an Aladdin lamp, in one hand, when suddenly, out of nowhere, what seemed like the world's hugest, coldest and clammiest frog came sailing through the air and landed on my bare shoulder! Only the grace of God and the knowledge that I could not spare my only light kept me from dropping the lamp and forced me to evict the frog from my shoulder the best way I could!

Like life anywhere, there were times of discouragement, physical exhaustion and soul-searching. But God graciously outweighed all of those with the wonderful experiences of living among the Asmat people.

When Dr. Dresser and his wife Sylvia were away, I was the only foreigner left on the mission station. However, the people made me feel loved and God's presence was so real that I did not feel lonely. On one occasion when the Dressers were going to be gone for a while, the local pastor, an Asmat man named Yakob, came by the house. He wanted to encourage me with these words, *"Nona, if you should get a snake in your house, just call me!"* I hadn't even thought of having a snake in my house until he mentioned it!

Yakob was also to leave me one of my most memorable and inspirational memories of life at Pirimapun.

During one two and a half week period of the Dressers' absence, my life was built primarily around caring for a little six-year old girl who had tuberculosis and was in a coma. She needed tube feedings and medication every eight hours and injections every twelve hours, and so my life and schedule were shaped by her needs. Two babies were also delivered during this time, one by kerosene lamp and one by flashlight, and miscellaneous other duties also demanded attention.

The little girl's father was extremely grateful and wanted to find a way to express his appreciation. One afternoon as I was taking a break down by the sea shore, where a cool breeze could almost always be found, he approached me. He had brought various food items, including a lot of nice bananas, which he wanted to give to me as his way of saying thank you. I had plenty of food on hand at that time and felt reluctant to accept his sacrificial gift. However, I also felt that it would be wrong to deny him the opportunity to express his gratitude, and so I accepted the food with thanks.

Shortly after this, I met Yakob at the Dressers' house. While the Dressers were away, I fed their cats and Yakob looked after their chickens. It occurred to me that perhaps Yakob and his family could use the food I had been given.

Approaching him, I said, "*Yakob, how's the food situation at your house?*" He looked at me with a grave expression in his eyes and said, "*Nona, we have nothing to eat at my house, and my little girl is crying because she is hungry.*" His ministry in the village had kept him from going to the jungle to get *sago*. He said that he had thought the young man who was living with them might have brought back some *sago* for the family, "*but he came back empty.*" Continuing, Yakob said, "*I thought of coming and asking you if you had any food you could spare. But I decided to ask <u>God</u> instead!*" Tears came to my eyes and joy to my heart! I explained that I had been given food that I did not need and would be glad for his family to have it.

God had heard the cry of His child. Unknown to the outside world, tucked away in a village that the world would have called primitive, <u>God</u> knew this man and responded to his faith, just as He had done for me so many times.

Truly it would be difficult to leave these people, but before long God would be catapulting me into new experiences as the Dresser family and I moved about seventy-five miles deeper into the jungle to begin a ministry at a place called Senggo.

SENGGO

Chapter 26

Not only was the actual moving of the small hospital and homes a herculean task, but also the question of *where* to relocate was a major decision. At the annual field conference in June 1971 — the time when the missionary family met to care for mission business — the need for further surveys was discussed. These would be made in consultation with the Missionary Aviation Fellowship.

Much of the south coast was swampy, and so we needed to search out a place with enough solid ground for construction. It was also important to find a location which could be serviced by both float planes and wheeled planes and centrally located to serve the greatest number of people. It should be accessible to other MAF routing in order to enable their ministry to work with us most efficiently and effectively. The Field Council and the Medical Committee were commissioned to make the final decision.

After a lot of thought, prayer and research, a

decision was reached on Monday, August 16, 1971. The new location would be at a place called Senggo, which was nestled in the jungle about seventy-five miles inland from Pirimapun. Senggo was surrounded by swamp, but the area itself was long enough for the building of an airstrip and also had enough solid ground for the building of a hospital and houses. The people there were of the Citak tribe. Work on clearing the area would be started as soon as possible. We hoped to be at least partially moved before the next high tide season.

Step by step the work was begun. Buildings were torn down at Pirimapun and transported to the new location at Senggo, where the wood and other usable materials would be utilized.

The Mother-Baby Clinic building and the store-room were among the first to come down, and then it was time to tear down my house. I moved into the hospital delivery room, where an IV stand consti-tuted my "clothes closet." With my two-burner kerosene stove and portable oven, I could fix my breakfasts there, and other meals would be taken with the Dressers at their house. A few days later, as the hospital was being torn down around me, I helped Sylvia Dresser clean out their son David's room so that I could move into it. By now, their house was also full of packing drums and boxes. I waxed poetic, writing of our experiences:

> *There were storms on the coast,*
> *So we weren't dry as toast*
> *And our station was fast going under.*
> *The waves they did splash*

And sure made us dash
To pack before stuff was asunder!

My own house I left,
Feeling sort of bereft,
And moved for a few days or more
To the hospital where
There was one room to spare
And from there to the Dressers' back door.

Into their house we packed
And the pace never slacked,
Making ready to move to the jungle.
With three cats and three boys
We had no lack for noise.
No telling what all we did bungle!

To add to the din,
Once a chicken got in,
Contributing to the confusion;
But days still progressed
And we were much blessed
In spite of life's rapid diffusion.

On Saturday, November 13, 1971, we made the big move! As there was not yet an airstrip at Senggo, we traveled by float plane, about forty-five minutes by air from Pirimapun. On the riverbank at Senggo, we climbed into a boat (not motorized) and traveled approximately forty-five minutes more. After that, a half-hour's walk through the jungle brought us to the first view of our new home – a temporary bush house, built in an area that had been cleared in dense jungle.

My poem continued:

> *At last the day came*
> *When we boarded a plane*
> *And up from the river we flew*
> *To a new place we know*
> *By the name of Senggo*
> *Somewhere out there in the blue!*
>
> *Getting out of the plane,*
> *Fortunately, without rain,*
> *Before us still lay a long trip.*
> *We boarded a boat,*
> *Down the river did float*
> *As oars in the water would dip.*
>
> *At the end of the ride*
> *There was still a big stride*
> *As we walked the first time through that*
> *jungle.*
> *Half hour more*
> *Almost to the door*
> *Home Sweet Home – be it ever so humble.*

As there was only one house, I continued living with Ken and Sylvia Dresser and their three boys, David, Andrew and George, until another bush house could be constructed. Our first overnight missionary guest was Field Chairman Ron Hill, who came for a visit about four days later.

I described my initial impressions of life at Senggo in a letter to friends back home.

"Our setting is almost too beautiful to be real! . . . Looking down the path and off into the jungle looks almost like looking at a painting, but the nice difference is that it's real! Tall, tall trees stand majestically with vines clinging to their trunks or hanging gracefully from their branches, and many of them have orchids. The orchids aren't blooming right now, but they should be beautiful when they are. There are some beautiful pink-red flowers blooming in the tops of some of the trees; I can't decide yet if they are growing on the tree or are a vine in the tree. There are some carnivorous plants, too, with green cup-shaped blossoms. They trap flies and bugs.

I've learned at last why Tarzan always swings through the jungle on vines! It must be because it's so difficult to walk! It means climbing over logs and tripping on vines and sinking down in soft spots, etc., but it's still fun. Ken and Field Chairman Ron Hill let me go with them down the "airstrip" the other day, and what a walk. I fell down shortly after we'd gotten out of our "front yard," but was more careful after that and didn't fall another time the whole trip – though the men had to give me a chance to catch up with them every once in a while or wait for me to pull stickers out of my shoes!

Water has been a bit of a problem. We have had a well dug, but can't tell for sure yet whether it'll work or not. There is a small water hole in the jungle, about five minutes walk behind our house (a beautiful trek!) and we are getting some water from that. . . . Ken and the three boys had their baths with a half bucket of water; I had about a third of a bucket all to myself, and there was at least that much left for Sylvia, who took her bath later!

On December 13, 1971, exactly a month after the Dressers and I arrived at Senggo, we were joined by a new missionary from Modoc, Indiana, Patricia Moore. Pat and I met for the first time on the riverbank at Senggo, when she alighted from the MAF float plane. Together we settled into a rowboat (which had no seats) on top of the boxes and suitcases, and began the forty-five minute trip down the narrow, winding river. At the end of the boat ride, a thirty-minute walk led to our temporary home. Since there was still only one house available, the Dresser family and the two of us all lived together in it for a while, with the number of occupants swelling to nine when the two oldest Dresser children, Mark and Jean, came home from the missionary children's boarding school in Sentani for the Christmas and New Year's vacation.

Though it was not quite finished, a bush house was made livable for Pat and me by the end of December, 1971. The floors needed work; there were no racks for hanging clothes, and a porch was yet to be built. The house was situated in an area which had been cleared out of virgin jungle by axes, large knives and manpower. It was located about a half-hour's walk from the Dressers' bush house. The distance between the houses was because of a change in plans for the location of the airstrip. In the green beauty of the jungle, rare and beautiful butterflies of many designs and bright colors flitted through the air. Admittedly, there was a lot of mud, as trees were removed, but it was more than compensated by the beauty of our surroundings.

Our house was made of native materials, with walls of *gaba-gaba* (large stems from *sago* palm tree leaves, which were several feet long and from one to three inches in width) and a thatched roof made of strips of leaves from *sago* palm trees. The main supporting beams were poles taken from the jungle, bark still on them and many with their green moss still there. They were held together by rattan, strengthened in some areas with nails. Windows were screened, but without glass. Walls did not reach the roof in some areas (there were no ceilings) and floors didn't quite reach the walls in others. The gaps were sufficient for mosquitos, flies, frogs and crawling creatures – even the cats, Blueberry and Muffin – to enter. One night I counted five large frogs sitting on the rafters as they serenaded us. At night we slept under mosquito nets and were careful to shine a flashlight on the floor before stepping out of bed in the dark.

Our floors were made of poles, overlaid with strips of palm tree bark from the jungle. In some areas we put down grass mats to serve as carpets. At first it felt as if we were walking on a trampoline, but such floors certainly had their advantages. Liquid spills were not a worry, when liquid could simply run through the floor. Some other spills were a little more challenging, however. One night I spilled my malaria pills and had to crawl under the house with a flashlight, hoping that I wouldn't meet any snakes in the process. I couldn't leave the pills there until the next morning, as they would have disintegrated in the humidity.

Lamps, iron, stove and refrigerator operated on kerosene. However, for the first seven or eight days we were without a fridge. Pat and I were not yet set up with drums or a water tank to catch rain water, so initially all our water had to be carried in buckets from a water hole in the jungle. The water was often the color of tea. We had to remember to boil the water from the water hole far enough ahead of time that it could cool down to room temperature — the coolest drink we could manage.

We had a shower room adjacent to the back porch. There was no shower or bath tub, of course, but a bucket served adequately. Our drain system was the floor, as in the remainder of the house. Pat came up with the idea of putting a door in the wall between the kitchen and the shower room. Thus we had the luxury of bathing without going outside and across the porch on our way to or from the shower.

The toilet was out in the back yard in its own little shed made of *gaba-gaba* and thatch, not too far from the house. A little distance was desirable for health's sake, as amoebiasis was very prevalent and flies were plentiful.

In order to avoid unnecessary weight for the airplane during our move, the Dressers and I had let our food supplies diminish before moving from Pirimapun to Senggo. We thought that we would replenish our supplies after getting to Senggo. But, as it turned out, the warehouse at the MAF base in Sentani was low on stock and so we were not able to purchase some staple goods for a while. Pat and I went out in the mornings and bought *kasbih* (a starchy root from which tapioca is made) from the local people, usually paying with fish hooks. We learned to cook *kasbih* in every way possible: baked, french fried, mashed – or any other way we could dream up. When flour was gone and we could no longer make bread, one morning we had cake for breakfast! The cake mix had been in a package received from the States.

But it was home, and Pat and I had some wonderful times of fellowship together. We shared the things that were on our hearts, and every day we had a time of Bible reading and prayer together. Pat, a registered medical technologist with special training in the field of tropical diseases at Mt. Sinai Hospital in Chicago did lab work on the back porch. I conducted a clinic on the front porch.

Pat and I laughingly talked of writing an article called, "P's and Q's of the Jungle," in which we would explain the need for balancing oneself on a log when a path disappeared, stopping to wash the mud from our feet when we found a water hole, and getting through what we called "Leech Lane." Leech

Lane was between our house and the village, an area through which it seemed almost impossible to pass without finding at least one of those blood-sucking snail-like creatures attached to a foot or leg afterward.

About a week after Pat's arrival, we went to a mountain station for Christmas. The climate was perfect there — not as cold as the higher elevations and not as hot as the jungle areas. There were six other single gals there and it was one big house party. We had a wonderful time.

Then another bush house was constructed beside ours and missionaries Larry and Shirley Rascher moved into it on February 5, 1972. We enjoyed their fellowship a lot.

Three days later, on February 8, 1972, the pregnant wife of one of the village teachers came to us in labor. After checking her and finding that everything appeared normal, I sent a carrier with a note to Dr. Dresser. His reply was *"Carry on!"* So she stayed with us at our house. As we had no other bed, I put her into my bed and stretched myself out on the chaise lawn chair that constituted part of our living room furniture. The little boy, their first child, was born about 10:40 p.m. Shirley had come over to observe and she held the kerosene lamp close while I helped the mother and Pat suctioned the baby.

Five days after that, Larry and Shirley's house burned to the ground while we were away at church. The fire took all their possessions, including the pictures of their two young children who had been lost at sea the previous July. If it had been any other day of the week, probably someone would have been around and perhaps something could have been salvaged.

With their house gone, Larry and Shirley came over to our house and we fixed lunch together. My heart was touched as Larry stood on the front porch looking over at the burning embers and began to sing the chorus of a song, "*I will serve Him because I love Him.*"

It was decided that it would be best for them to go to Yaosakor that afternoon, so Dr. Dresser contacted the Missionary Aviation Fellowship pilot and made the arrangements. At Yaosakor, they could stay temporarily in the home of Bob and Doris Frazier who were away at the time.

The jungle seemed strangely silent that night. In the short time they had been next door, we had grown accustomed to having someone else around, to seeing the lamplight in their windows and hearing their uplifting music floating through the night air.

On Tuesday, February 15, 1972, Bob and Amber Leland arrived to begin life as missionaries at Senggo. Our staff was growing!

We thought we were settling in, planning for and getting started in our new lives and ministries at Senggo. Unknown to me, my life was about to change and my journey to continue. A new location and a completely different ministry lay ahead sooner than I would ever have imagined!

On Friday, February 18, 1972, Field Chairman Ron Hill visited Senggo and informed us that the field council was requesting that I move to the field headquarters in Manokwari and assume bookkeeping responsibilities when the Hills left for furlough. I had never been a bookkeeper and math had never been my first love! But when God leads, He enables – even when it comes to keeping books in American dollars, Australian dollars and Indonesian Rupiahs.

Pat was to have gone to Agats on February 29, 1972, to begin Indonesian language study, but her flight was delayed one day. Early that same afternoon, a strong wind blew our thatched roof partially off, leaving about half of the roof standing upright instead of lying down! Workers fixed it, and we dried the furniture and hung the floor mats out to dry.

The next day, March 1, Shirley Rascher arrived back at Senggo. Shirley, Larry and I were to share our house until I left for Manokwari in about a week and then it would be theirs. Later that day we accompanied Pat to the river for her flight. Another tropical rain hit as we walked back home through the jungle and Shirley and I were drenched with rain. When we arrived at the house, the roof was partially off and it was raining in again! Larry arrived on March 2.

Faith is not following God only when the path lies through the jungle or some other physically difficult place. It is also obedience when He leads back to the city.

MANOKWARI

Chapter 27

My journey from the jungle to the city was a trip to be remembered! There were no roads from Senggo to anywhere, and as yet there was no airstrip at Senggo, which meant that traveling out of Senggo by plane was not an option.

On March 7, 1972, Shirley and Larry Rascher, Bob Leland, helpers with boxes, suitcases and I began our parade through the jungle. When we arrived at the river, the water level was down so low that it was necessary to use a canoe for the first part of the journey. This meant that there was not enough room for everyone and so goodbyes were said to Shirley and Bob at the river bank. I went the rest of the way with Larry and the Irianese boys who were paddling the canoe. A number of times it was necessary to climb out of the canoe and stand on a log in the river or on the mucky river bank, alert for crocodiles, as they maneuvered the canoe over a log or a fallen tree. At one point we encountered a log and a curve in the river at the same time and Larry, fully clothed and standing up in back of the boat rowing, was knocked overboard. Fortunately for me, I was sitting down holding onto the sides of the canoe. Typical of Larry, he rose to the river's surface laughing!

There was a little rain off and on, but I had an umbrella with me. When we reached a larger river, we changed from the canoe to a motor boat and traveled the next part of the journey in more luxurious fashion – I sat on a tow sack! Eventually we arrived at the biggest river, the one where the float plane would land, and waited for the plane.

Finally I was aboard the MAF float plane and on my way to Yaosakor, where I would spend the night at the home of TEAM missionaries Bob and Doris Frazier. My flight arrived about 3:00 p.m. and Doris had a hot meal ready for me. That was greatly appreciated as I hadn't had anything to eat since early that morning.

Bob wanted me to examine several pregnant women in the clinic that he operated at Yaosakor. They came about 4:00 p.m. and we finished about 5:30. While doing the prenatal examinations, I began experiencing abdominal pain and diarrhea. Bob gave me some medicine for it and I was okay by the next morning.

The following morning, March 8, 1972, I started out in a wheeled plane headed for Sentani and eventually on to Manokwari. However, about 25 minutes out of Yaosakor we had to turn back. There was a medical emergency on a south coast mission station and the missionaries radioed the pilot as they were unable to make contact with either Yaosakor to request a flight or Senggo to talk with the doctor. When we arrived back over Yaosakor, they were rolling drums of fuel across the airstrip, and so we had to circle the airstrip until they got it cleared off. Then we needed to land and refuel, due to the extra flying. Finally we left again and flew to Wamena, where I changed planes and flew on to Sentani.

Thursday, March 9, 1972, my first glimpse of Manokwari came into view. Having entered West Irian through Sentani and the capital city of Jayapura I had not visited TEAM's field headquarters previously. But now I was here, ready to become better acquainted with missionaries Ron and Charlene Hill and to learn the ropes prior to their leaving Manokwari for furlough on July 8.

It had been decided that Larry and Shirley Rascher would also be transferred to Manokwari while the Hills were on furlough. Larry was in charge of the Manokwari station, and Shirley immediately started Bible classes with the Indonesian-speaking ladies and Sunday school classes with the neighborhood children. I was delighted to live next door to them once again.

Manokwari was a small coastal town and, unlike the primitive interior and south coast, it had felt the impact of the outside world. Its people were a conglomerate of both educated and illiterate. People who passed by on the street were mixed in their apparel from sarongs and oriental long skirts with long-sleeved overblouses to boys with the latest western style pants and girls in mini skirts. There was no television, but people listened to the radio and were influenced by movies. A limited selection of secular magazines in the Indonesian language was available.

In contrast to the jungle, where the only modes of transportation were walking, traveling by canoe or flying, here there were bicycles, motorcycles and cars. Freighters docked across the street from TEAM's headquarters, sometimes from as far away as Jakarta and Singapore.

Life seemed luxurious with a solid floor beneath my feet and running water (cold only, of course, but running water nonetheless!). To be more accurate, I should add that it wasn't always running; sometimes the city turned it off all day without any warning. On one occasion, the water was turned off for a long time while I had overnight missionary guests. Bathing, flushing the toilet and washing dishes for a house full of us was quite a challenge. When I ran out of clean dishes and could wash no more, I went next door and borrowed dishes from Shirley!

The local electric current was normally turned off by the city for a few hours each day, but sometimes it also went off at unexpected hours. However, when it was on, it was certainly a step forward over a kerosene lamp!

Sunday was different, too. Instead of walking through the jungle to get to church, while watching for snakes and stopping to balance myself on a log or wash my muddy feet in a jungle water hole, I rode down a paved street. Instead of a church building with a dirt floor and with dogs and pigs running in and out, the building where we met had doors, windows and a floor. As was customary, there were two sections of backless benches. Men sat on one side and ladies on the other.

I was pleasantly surprised to find so many of the lush tropical plants and trees that I had loved in the jungle growing in the Manokwari area. There was a beautiful beach nearby with clean sand that was almost white. The water was a lovely aqua, the color of many artificially colored pools in the States and as clear as glass! We could swim in it, too. (Although we had lived on the beach at Pirimapun, we could not swim there because of poisonous snakes and stinging fish.) Alongside the beach and not far from the water, beautiful shade trees stood majestically with split philodendron vines climbing their trunks.

Medical work was not completely left behind. In May there was a cholera epidemic in our area. We were without any cholera vaccine, but the Hills were in Sentani and were able to bring a bottle home with them when they returned to Manokwari. I gave injections to Ron, Charlene, their daughter Nancy, and the Irianese family who worked for them. Then the question arose as to who would give me my injection! I said there had to be a first time for everyone and that I would teach someone how to do it. Finally Field Chairman Ron Hill gave it to me. He really did a nice job; it didn't hurt a bit!

One morning at precisely 4:30 a.m. I was awakened by the male voice of a man who worked for the Raschers. Outside my bedroom window, he called softly but with a note of urgency, "*Nona, my wife is sick*!" Instantly I was awake and alert. I recognized his voice and knew that he meant his wife was in labor. Checking her a few minutes later, I confirmed that she definitely was in labor. Settling her into my guest room, I sent her husband to call an Irianese friend who was a trained and very capable midwife. They arrived within half an hour; by then we had a handsome baby boy waiting to welcome them! I had called Shirley Rascher from her house next door around 5:00 a.m. God blessed us with a good delivery and a healthy baby. There was no running water at that time, but — after a long dry spell — our first rain occurred simultaneously with the arrival of this little boy. Dashing out with a bucket, I caught rain water as it gushed off the roof! When the midwife arrived, I turned over the mother to her while I bathed and dressed the new baby. Shirley went next door to her home to prepare breakfast for all of us.

Another facet of our ministry was of course with the local church. Sunday mornings found an average of twenty-five preschoolers and maybe a few first graders making their way to my house for an 8:00 a.m. Sunday school. I could expect them to start gathering in my front yard any time after 7:00, where they played until I opened the door and called them to come in for Sunday school.

Shirley conducted a class for older children at the same time in their home, and Larry taught an adult class at the church. Following Sunday school, we went to the church for the Sunday morning worship service, which often lasted anywhere from one and a half to two hours. In the afternoon there was choir practice, usually involving from two to three hours, and in the evening a worship service was held in someone's home (alternating homes from week to week).

It was a busy year filled with the challenge of bookkeeping and many other events. The months rolled by quickly and then it was time for the Hills to return to the field. It was also time for me to plan next steps. With Charlene returning and resuming the bookkeeping in July, what should I do next?

Moving in Irian Jaya was slow and expensive. If I returned to the south coast, it would probably take so long to get my stuff there that by the time I got moved and settled into a ministry it would be time to start packing for furlough. So it seemed wise that I should go ahead and plan to leave the field for furlough a few months early. This decision was confirmed by the fact that I had some health problems and after the mission doctor examined me he advised that I not delay my departure beyond mid-August.

After some busy days of packing and trying to finish what seemed like a million miscellaneous tasks, August 12, 1973, found me boarding an Indonesian airline. I was not headed to the USA, however, but rather to Rhodesia, Africa!

On learning that they needed help in the office, I had hoped to spend up to three months in Rhodesia before traveling on to the USA. However, Dr. Ken

Dresser would only grant medical clearance for a two-week visit. I needed surgery and was to be admitted to the hospital in Memphis, Tennessee, shortly after arriving back in the States. Enjoyable and restful overnight stops en route were required and paid for by the airlines in both Bombay, India, and Nairobi, Kenya. What a thrill it was to land in Salisbury once again on the night of August 15 and to be met with a warm welcome by Rhodesian TEAM-Mates!

My two weeks in Rhodesia were a wonderful time of reunion with many friends. I was able to visit almost all the mission stations and missionaries for at least a short time. I even had the opportunity to get in on part of a *ruwadzano* (a week-end conference for African ladies) and to share in one of their African meals of *sadza* (thick corn meal porridge) and beans.

It was good to view the progress of the mission and of Rhodesia itself. TEAM Rhodesia now had a lovely modern office, replacing the old one, as well as several other new buildings plus improvements on older buildings. It was nice, too, to find many things still the same so that the enjoyment of progress was mingled with enough familiarity that I felt right at home.

I was shy about using the Shona language beyond greetings, as my language skills felt quite rusty after five years of disuse. But day by day I was able to understand more and by the end of my stay was willing to attempt a bit of conversation.

Then it was time to say farewell to Rhodesia,

board a 747 jet to London and continue my journey back to the USA. My second term of missionary service was now complete and new challenges would be mine in the months ahead.

WHEATON

Chapter 28

It was Wednesday evening, August 29, 1973, when I once again said goodbye to Rhodesia and flew to London en route to New York and then on to Arkansas. The plane was late leaving London, which caused me to miss the connection from New York to Arkansas. The airline provided hotel accommodations overnight in New York and I was glad to have the opportunity to rest up a bit before flying on to Arkansas.

Then, after spending some time with my family in Arkansas, I traveled on to Memphis, TN, on Saturday, September 15, via Greyhound bus. On arrival there, I was met at the bus station in Memphis by Lorene and Bill Overway and also former professors at MSBC, Paul and Dorothy Davidson. Lorene and Bill had arranged that a large group would not be there to meet me, as they correctly assumed that I was too exhausted for a lot of socializing. I stayed with Lorene and Bill in their home for a few days and on September 18 was admitted to the Baptist Memorial Hospital in Memphis. Dr. Andrews came by my hospital room and said he was considering delaying my surgery a day or two to build me up. He was awaiting lab reports. Evidently the lab reports were sufficiently good, as surgery (an abdominal hysterectomy) was performed on schedule on September 19, 1973. After the operation I began to go into shock and my blood pressure dropped to 70/40. The doctor was called back to the hospital and for a few days I was kept in bed with my feet elevated. On September 27 I was discharged from the hospital and later that day Bill and Lorene took me to the airport. I flew back to Fort Smith, where my parents and my sister Dolores were waiting at the airport.

By early October, I was on my way back to Wheaton. By the latter part of the month I was working part-time in the TEAM's international headquarters office.

Life found me contrasting my two worlds. Things so normal in the past now impressed me:

- *the smoothness of paved airstrips and the cleanliness of shining floors in public places.*
- *feeling a little out of place among so many white people.*
- *lying in a hospital bed in a beautiful, well-equipped building and remembering those suffering elsewhere with none of these things.*
- *having fun with Christian friends and becoming suddenly aware of how much I had missed this fellowship.*

- *marveling at flour that didn't have to be sifted fifteen times before use and sugar that was clean and fine-grained. Pure water (hot, too!) At the touch of a tap.*
- *thinking of those overseas who had become very dear and missing them so much that the tears came.*
- *the luxury of a bath tub. The pleasure of a glass of fresh milk.*
- *attending worship services in my own language. Being overwhelmed with the beauty of instrumental music.*
- *missing the simple Indonesian services in our backless-benched and piano-less church building.*
- *looking to God for His leading and timing in whatever lay ahead.*

What did lie ahead? In January, 1974, while in Memphis, TN, for a missions conference, I returned to the surgeon for a checkup. He seemed satisfied that I would be able to return to Irian Jaya. But just four days later, back in Wheaton something new entered the picture!

On January 29, 1974, Rolf Egeland, TEAM's administrative secretary, called me into his office and talked with me about needs there. He asked me to consider staying on permanently as a part of the home staff. Earlier he had mentioned that if I could not get medical clearance for a return to Irian Jaya (the name West Irian had been changed to Irian Jaya in 1973) the administrative staff would like me to consider such an assignment. But now the invitation was to stay was extended even if medical clearance was received.

Sometimes it seems so difficult to know God's will. I know that there are those who insist that it's always simple and that if you *really want* to do His will you will know what it is. I do not agree that it is always so simple. Sometimes it is. There *are* times when He lays a step so clearly on our hearts that there can be no doubt. I had experienced that many times. But on some occasions, my heart sincerely wanted more than anything else to do what He wanted and yet I was pulled in different directions, not knowing which was the right course. This was one of those times.

Both directions seemed good. Should I stay at the international headquarters and share in serving *all* the fields – or did God want me to return to a ministry in Irian Jaya? Serving in a capacity that affected only one small corner of the world would be enough, if that was what God wanted.

The secret element entering the picture and making the decision especially difficult was that— although I had never mentioned it to anyone — I had long felt that at some point in time God wanted me to serve with the home staff. Now I had been invited to do so. But was this the right time? It looked as if I would obtain medical clearance and would also be able to obtain another visa for Irian Jaya. These were the two obstacles that had blocked my going there for many years. Now they no longer stood in the way.

Logic and my heart wrestled with each other.

Maybe I should go overseas again and trust God to make another opening for me in the home office at a later date. Or should I accept that His leading in the past, coupled with what was happening now, was sufficient guidance?

By mid February, trying to look at things objectively and disentangle facts from emotions, I told the administrative staff that I thought the Lord was leading me to accept the assignment at headquarters. This was not yet made public, as it was necessary for them to contact the field leaders in Irian Jaya before making an official announcement. The first week in April a reply came from the field chairman in Irian Jaya saying that they wanted me to return to the field if my health permitted, rather than be assigned to the home office.

I had thought it likely that the field leaders would simply agree that it was fine for me to stay in Wheaton, or that it didn't really matter much to them one way or the other. Perhaps that would provide the confirmation of which I felt so sorely in need. Now it was totally back to me. What answer would I, should I, give? This conflict filled almost every waking thought for months.

At the annual conference in May, 1974, the Medical Director of the Mission, Dr. Andrew Karsgaard, said that He wasn't ready to give total medical clearance at that point. It would be necessary to extend my furlough a bit, even if I were to return to the field. Perhaps I was to stay home and help in the home office for several months and then return to Irian Jaya, thus in a way fulfilling both options!

Finally my decision was made. Based on the previous leading regarding working with the home staff, I felt I must simply act in faith and accept the assignment. After a few more days of waiting – and mustering up the courage to say it – I shared this with Deputation Secretary Nolan Balman, with whom I was working, then with Rolf Egeland and later with Carl Davis, the Far East Secretary.

Strangely, there was no immediate rush of peace within me. On the contrary, that night or shortly thereafter I awoke in the middle of the night and was hit with the reality that I had cut myself off from return to Irian Jaya. Such despair overwhelmed me that I fell to my knees beside the bed and cried out to the Lord. I crawled back into bed and fell asleep and when I awoke in the morning it was with a sweet sense of peace. God knew the intent of my heart.

Sometimes it seemed that I had peace for a while, perhaps out of the feeling that I had tried to be obedient. Other times I felt numb about the whole thing. My thoughts ranged from, *"should I have waited for some further confirmation before accepting a permanent assignment to the home office?"* to *"did the Lord want me to go back for another term before staying here?"* Were my emotions of love and longing for that land and its people being confused with a lack of peace?

I enjoyed my work at TEAM headquarters and became very close to wonderful coworkers there. However, the continuing struggle was never far from my thoughts and prayers. More than a year passed. The need for missionaries in Irian Jaya appeared even more critical. My dear friend Jennifer Berry, who was a very qualified nurse, had applied for a visa to serve in Irian Jaya. But on June 17, 1975, we received word that it was refused. Several new missionary appointees were heading toward Irian Jaya. But it would be a while before they could actually go, and even then it would be another six months or so before they could finish initial language study and get into the work.

These facts and the continuing confusion within my heart led me to talk with Far East Secretary Carl Davis about the possibility of returning to Irian Jaya and what he felt about the wisdom of such a move. A fresh peace and liberty began returning to me. Mr. Davis and I agreed to ask the Lord for an answer by August 15.

On August 15, 1975, my decision was given: I would return to Irian Jaya if the Lord continued to lead and confirm this action. Even though there would be difficulties to face in following through on this decision my heart was filled with peace and joy. My parents were disappointed and very unhappy about my plans to go back overseas, and my heart ached to have to hurt them.

I continued working full time in the TEAM office through December 31, 1975. Then the whirlwind of preparation began – visits to family and friends and supporting churches, disposing of furniture, shopping, packing, inoculations and travel arrangements. Tentative plans to leave for Irian Jaya at the end of January, 1976, were delayed by a missing letter required for my visa application. However, a replacement letter came through with amazing speed and then the visa application was filed immediately. It was placed in the mail on January 27 and a cable advising that it had been granted was received by the TEAM office within less than three weeks, on Monday, February 16!

Perhaps God had gone to special lengths to grant me assurance that returning to Irian Jaya really was His will. I would need that confirmation before many months had passed.

RETURN

Chapter 29

There was no opportunity for a lingering farewell look at Chicago. Scarcely had the jet taken off, before the clouds of a rainy afternoon cut it off from view. It was March 30, 1976, and I was on my way back to Irian Jaya.

My assignment for this term was Manokwari, where I had been asked to serve as secretary to the field chairman and also to continue in other church-related ministries as in my previous term. However, because of a shortage of medical staff, I was to go to Senggo first and help out at the hospital for a few months. A new missionary nurse, Ruth Dougherty, was in language study and after completing that she would replace me at Senggo.

At the airport in Los Angeles I was met by Ruth Moberg, who took me to her apartment for the night. Her sister Nancy Simmons and Nancy's husband Jim came over for a visit, as well as friends Tom and Carol Herron, all part of my former church family at

Eleventh Street Baptist in Los Angeles.

My overseas flight, originally scheduled for departure from Los Angeles at 9:00 a.m. the following morning, was delayed for a few hours and finally took off about 2:00 p.m. But at last I was on my way back, stopping only where the airline schedules required: Honolulu, Tokyo, Hong Kong, Bangkok, Singapore, Jakarta, Masassar, Biak and finally Sentani, Irian Jaya. After many wearying hours of travel, I was grateful for the required overnight stop in Bangkok and ready for the hot bath and good rest provided in an air conditioned hotel room. After that it was necessary to stop in Jakarta, where two nights were spent at the missionary guest house before an ongoing flight to Biak was available.

The last required overnight stop was on the small island of Biak, only about an hour and a half from Sentani by air. I stayed in the hotel and that in itself was quite an experience!

Settling into my hotel room in Biak, I discovered that neither toilet tissue, soap, nor washcloth were provided. The bath towel, originally red and white, was now red and grey. There were no clothes hangers or hooks in the wooden wardrobe which served as a closet, and the wardrobe door hung open because I couldn't get it to stay closed. There was no lock on the window of the ground floor room.

On the bed the bottom sheet looked as it if hadn't been laundered since the previous (how many?) occupant(s). There was no top sheet, but there was a bedspread. A welcoming party of tiny insects of some sort quickly arrived and began swarming over my suitcases. They were soon joined by huge tropical roaches! While I went to the dining room, I left my briefcase open and when I returned found that a big cockroach had made itself at home in a manila envelope left open in the briefcase. He was quickly evicted!

I couldn't quite bring myself to undress and lie down on the smelly bed in a clean gown. I had undressed and bathed earlier, during the hot afternoon, but things seemed so much creepier after dark! I knew that I must try to get some rest, though, and so decided to just take off my dress and lie down on top of the bedspread. It was a cool, rainy night. I pulled the blanket up over me but was kept awake by its odor and so decided to use my lightweight coat over my body and the blanket over my feet.

Lifting my heart to God I said from the bottom of it, *"Lord, I'm lying here because I love You."* Obedience to God's will had brought me to this place and His peace flooded my being. Remembering that He had done so much for me, the realization swept over me that my little "sacrifice" was nothing by comparison, and I told Him so. His love was very sweet and precious in that moment before I slipped off to sleep.

A fresh new day was dawning as I checked into the Biak airport around 5:00 a.m. on April 6, 1976, for the last lap of my journey from Chicago to Sentani — a distance that stretched halfway around the world.

Actually, I had hoped to bypass Sentani and go to Manokwari instead, and then from there on to

Senggo. In the Sentani area, a contagious hepatitis-like disease called the "Sentani Bug" was spreading and I hoped to avoid it. I seem to have a penchant for attracting tropical diseases. The "Sentani Bug" was being researched with the hope of finding a cause and a cure, but both of those had continued to elude the medical team.

However, it was not possible to avoid Sentani, as clearance by the local government in the nearby capital city of Jayapura was required. That was granted a week later, on Thursday, April 15. Then there was a wait of five more days before a flight was available, and so it was Tuesday, April 20, 1976, when I reached my final destination — Senggo.

Only by a good stretch of the imagination or actually having been there could one fathom that this was the same place where Ken and Sylvia Dresser and I had moved just a few years before! Instead of a small clearing in dense jungle where we had lived in a thatched roof house, used swamp water and walked two hours round trip to meet the plane at the river, now there was a vast cleared area! Not only was it cleared, but grassy with flowers and palm trees. There were four solidly built homes with a fifth nearing completion, plus a well-designed hospital and a huge airstrip! The airstrip had been enlarged and maintained by an oil exploration group in the area, and the Indonesian government had built offices just across the airstrip from the hospital.

The next day I was given a tour of the new hospital and a brief reorientation to medical work. That night Dr. Dresser delivered a baby, face presentation and thus difficult, for a lady with kidney stones and pyelonephritis. I was his only helper, as his wife Sylvia was convalescing from hepatitis. Scurrying around I tried to find things, to figure out how to use the new autoclave and how to sterilize the instruments that he needed..

As the days passed and things settled down, I helped where needed. I did secretarial work relative to the medical program, washed bottles, counted pills, worked with the mother and baby clinic, and helped entertain missionary patients and other guests, along with doing some Indonesian language study. The current missionary staff consisted of Ken and Sylvia Dresser and their children, plus Jerald and Esther Peter (on loan from another mission to help with construction) and their children Jeanne, Janet and Jerry. Bob and Amber Leland arrived back from furlough two days after I got to Senggo. The days and nights were full as we seemed to move from one crisis to another in the medical work.

June 12 had been a sunny day and I had failed to find a cloud in the sky. Although we had a lot of rain when I first came to Senggo in April, lately there had been very little. Since our water supply depended on the rain, things were getting rather serious. I had been out of drinking water and had gotten some from the hospital and some from the Dressers, who had a large tank. I had some empty oil drums outside to catch water that could be used for washing clothes, bathing, and flushing the toilet, etc. However, even that source of supply was very low and I was practically scraping the bottom to get enough water for a bath. I limited what I used for bathing and used part of it to flush the toilet. Supper dishes were piled up with the hope that there might be more water by morning. I realized that without rain it would also be necessary to wait a while before washing any more clothes.

I was not the only one low on water, of course. The local people had been feeling it, too, and even at the hospital some of the faucets failed to produce water that day.

As I prepared to brush my teeth with some of the drinking water hauled from the Dressers' house, I prayed, *"Father, could you send at least a little rain tonight? Nevertheless, have your will because I know that will be best."* I had prayed for rain before in recent days, although the situation had not been as desperate as it was that night.

Then as I began to brush my teeth, only a minute or two later I heard the incredible sound of rain! I didn't know that there were even any rain clouds around, since it had been hot and sunny all day.

My heart was thrilled – and so were my neighbors. As the Irianese living closest to me ran out of their house whooping and rejoicing, I also went out onto the steps and rejoiced silently, thanking God for providing – not just a little, not just enough to wash dishes, but an abundant downpour that within half an hour or less had wonderfully replenished the thirsty water drums!

Before going to bed, I heated water and washed up the dishes (including mixing bowls, measuring cups, etc., from the afternoon's baking), scoured the sink, rinsed the dishcloth in the fresh water and filled two tea kettles with water. Two buckets were also filled with water from the roof. *"Thank you, Father!"*

Saturday morning, June 26, had a dramatic beginning. About 4:30 a.m. I was awakened by the rough shaking of my bed – and of the whole house! It was an earthquake! The ironing board fell over with a bang and the kitchen sounded as if everything was crashing down. Jumping out of bed, I got into a housecoat and lit the kerosene lamp, but before I managed to go outside the quaking had subsided. The dishes must have only been banging against each other in the cupboard, as I found only one pitcher and two bottles on the floor afterward.

I learned later that the hardest hit area was approximately 90 miles from Senggo, at a place called Bime. There was quite a lot of damage there. We continued to feel after tremors at Senggo for a few days.

On Monday, July 5, 1976, having finished the initial course of Indonesian language study, Ruth Dougherty arrived at Senggo. She was ready to take up her duties as a missionary nurse at the hospital. We lived together for the remainder of my time there.

A dream came true on July 14, 1976, when I had the privilege of making a trip back to Pirimapun, where I had served during my first term in Irian Jaya. My heart was overwhelmed with gratitude to the Lord as once again I reveled in the beauty of the Cook River and its jungle. A national coworker, Dominggus Mayor, his twelve-year-old daughter

Yusi and fourteen-year-old Janet Peter went with me. Since there was no airstrip at Pirimapun, we flew to a now unstaffed mission station called Saman, the nearest location with an airstrip. There Yusi, Janet and I climbed into a dugout canoe to continue our journey to Pirimapun, about an hour and a half by canoe.

It was thrilling to be back at Pirimapun and to be reunited with loved ones there, including Martina, her husband Asut and baby Willem. Their other babies had died, but they were expecting another. Martina's father was also there, along with Martina's brother Willem and his wife Sai. What a joy it was to visit with many others from my days there, including Yakob, his wife Akan, and their little Dina. Their other babies had died. In addition to visiting, I set up a rudimentary clinic and began some medical work. The people thronged around most of the time from daybreak until bedtime.

Dominggus stayed at Saman, and Yusi, Janet and I at Pirimapun. The three of us set up temporary living quarters in a deserted government building, and slept on the floor with a mosquito net around us. We cooked over an open fire behind the building, using supplies that we had brought with us from Senggo. There was no electricity, of course. When we turned on a flashlight at night we could see that the walls had become alive with typically huge tropical roaches!

On Friday night I awoke around midnight with a chill that turned into fever. Not long thereafter, I began having chills and fever almost continuously, plus a left-sided sore throat and swollen gland and right-sided swelling in the groin. As I lay there in the dark alternating between chills and fever, I was physically miserable, but at the same time was filled with awe as I marveled at the tremendous peace that flooded my heart. It was the kind of peace that comes from a sense of His presence and the assurance of knowing that you are in the center of God's will.

Realizing that an increasingly elevated temperature could possibly result in a loss of consciousness and not wanting the girls to panic, I tried to prepare them for that possibility. I instructed them that if I should happen to pass out they should remain calm and just bathe my face with cool water. If that had happened, fourteen-year-old Janet would have been stranded since she did not speak Indonesian and Yusi could not speak English. But they were real troopers, and thankfully I remained conscious and alert.

We had no radio or any other way to communicate with the outside world from Pirimapun. But in the providence of God, Dominggus had come to Pirimapun on Friday. That Saturday morning he was able to take over the medical work and then get us back to Saman by canoe. On Saturday morning my temperature, which normally ran between 97 and 98 degrees, was 103. By 5:30 Sunday morning it still hovered at 102 degrees. There was a two-way radio at Saman and so Dominggus and I were able to communicate with Dr. Dresser from there. Without being able to examine me and from a distance, it was difficult for him to make a diagnosis. He said that it might be septicemia and asked Dominggus to give me a penicillin injection. I had planned to cut the ribbon to the new church building in Saman that Sunday morning, but since I was too weak to go, Janet cut it in my place. On Monday, July 18, the MAF plane picked us up at Saman and returned us to Senggo. Ruth had a nice clean bed ready for me.

The Field Council requested that I arrive in Manokwari by the first of September. So, on Thursday, August 26, 1976, it was time to turn over the medical ministry to Ruth, to say farewell to the south coast and head northward.

RESCUE

Chapter 30

As we flew northward toward our destination, the small town of Manokwari in the Bird's Head area of Irian Jaya, the weather was bad almost all the way. For a while we were lost in the air as the small Cessna aircraft found its way through clouds and sought to stay above mountain peaks. Perhaps these were symbolic of the mountain peaks and clouds that lay just ahead in my life. We were certainly grateful when we safely reached our destination: Manokwari, my new home.

The local missionary staff welcomed me, and Shirley Rascher took me grocery shopping so that I could begin to get settled. Charlene and Ron Hill invited me to their home for supper that evening.

A new office had been built during the two and a half years that I was in the States, and the new two-story building included a cozy apartment upstairs. It had two bedrooms, one bathroom, a living room and a kitchen/dining area which opened onto a small balcony. A view of the bay with the mountains in the distance beyond it created a breathtakingly beautiful scene. I was not feeling completely up to par, as I had continued to run a low grade fever following the illness at Pirimapun in July. But it felt good to begin settling into what I expected to be my home for a long time.

The following Monday was August 30, 1976, and it was my first day of work in the mission office. At lunch time, Ron and Charlene closed up the office and headed up the hill to their home for lunch and I went upstairs to the apartment to prepare mine. As I was getting things going on the little two-burner kerosene stove in my kitchen, there was a knock at the door. It was the inside door, the one on the second-floor landing of the stairway which connected the office below and the apartment above. Leaving the kitchen and crossing the small living room, I opened the door. There stood the office handyman, Piet (pronounced Pete).

I had met him for the first time shortly after my arrival in Manokwari a few days earlier. He worked for the mission and had been polite and helpful.

As he stood in the open doorway, he explained that the reason for his visit was that he had several passages of Scripture he wanted me to explain to him. He showed me the sheet of paper on which he had written several Bible references. Knowing that it would not be appropriate for me to entertain him alone in my apartment, I responded that it would be best to wait until the next morning and let Ron help him with this. But he was very insistent and showed no signs of leaving. Finally I told him frankly that I didn't think Ron would like his being in the apartment when I was alone in the building and that he must wait and talk with either Larry or Ron. However, when he still refused to leave, I finally agreed to go over just one of the Bible verses with him, hoping that would satisfy his immediate need. When I did, he laughed. That struck me as a strange reaction. Then I excused myself, left him momentarily, and went to the kitchen to turn off the heat under the food I was cooking.

As I returned to the living room, my whole world changed in a flash. That was when, shortly thereafter, I found myself lying on the bathroom floor thinking, *"What an ugly way to die,"* and hearing God's loving response, *"You are not going to die now!"*

The yard around the office was fenced. Before coming to my apartment, Piet had locked the gate to keep anyone from entering the grounds and thus insure his privacy. But God in His overruling sovereignty used that very action as a means of providing help for me!

Missionary Larry Rascher had left his motorcycle at the office and around 2:00 p.m. he came by to pick it up. If the gate had been unlocked, Larry would simply have gotten on his motorcycle and left. Instead, it was necessary for him to call up to my apartment and ask me to come down and unlock the gate. What a wonderful sound it was to hear his voice calling my name!

Since my initial screams for help, Piet had intermittently kept one of his strong hands clamped firmly over my mouth. But God ordained that at the moment Larry called my name from outside the fence, my mouth was free. With all the last bits of strength I could muster, I called to him for help.

I was still pinned down on the bathroom floor. As I lay limp on the floor, unable to move, Piet had managed to remove the remainder of his clothing. Our bodies were slippery from perspiration in that small space without air conditioning or a fan on a tropically hot afternoon. My hair was as wet with perspiration as if I had been in the shower.

We believe that God gave supernatural strength for the events that followed. Larry came over the fence in a flash. Even so, he didn't know where I was and the entire building was locked, so he called out, "*Where are you?*" Once again my mouth was covered, but managing to work my lips away from my teeth, I bit my captor on the hand a time or two. With my mouth temporarily free, I screamed out the word "*bathroom!*" "*Which bathroom?*" Larry wondered, perplexed. There were three in the building, including the one in my apartment. At first he thought that maybe I was in the office bathroom. Somehow he managed to find a way to climb up and look into that bathroom through a window. Finding it empty, he came bounding up the outside stairs to my apartment and literally burst through the locked door!

Wood splintering as the apartment door gave way under the impact of his charge – the sound of rescue – was one of the most welcome sounds I have ever heard. Moments later Larry's face appeared in the bathroom doorway. He grabbed my assailant, freed me from his grip, and sent me into my bedroom to lie down. As there was no phone in the apartment, Larry turned to bystanders who had followed him into the apartment and asked them to guard Piet while he went downstairs to the office to call Ron, Charlene and Shirley to come.

Ron and Charlene insisted that I go home with them, even though I felt I would be all right in my apartment now that it was over. To me, it seemed that I had come very close to being raped, but that he had not fully succeeded. My mind and emotions were not yet ready to accept the reality of what had happened.

The police sent a doctor to the Hills' home, and although it was about an hour and a half after the attack when he saw me, my pulse was still 140. The local people said that if Larry had not arrived in time, I would have been murdered.

I had not realized how badly I was injured, but by the next day there was hardly a space on my body that was not black and blue. I needed help to dress and comb my hair and could hardly walk for a few days. Scratches on my face became infected. My upper lip was swollen and for several days I had difficulty opening my mouth wide enough to eat. One scalp wound became infected, and Shirley cut my hair from around it (about 1" x 1-1/4"), scrubbed it with Phisophex and applied some medicine.

Almost two months later, on Monday, October 25, I received a summons to appear before the Indonesian judge the next morning. On arrival, I was glad to find that the judge with whom I would be in conference was a lady. We had a private conversation, talking for an hour or so, during which time I had an opportunity to share a bit of my Christian testimony with her. The judge said that the authorities were puzzled because Piet's own confession was worse than the charges I had brought against him. I was mystified and somewhat shaken as I listened to her read part of the descriptive statement of confession. He had told them that he had not only raped me once, but was attempting to do it the second time when Larry stopped him! Why would he tell a story like that? I was amazed!

At first, I thought that perhaps it was braggadocio on his part, rather than admitting failure. But with his life — or at least his future — hanging in the balance, it seemed a strange time to brag. Another explanation might be that because of his mental state at the time, he believed it happened as he had stated. The third possibility — and the most troubling to me — was that because of shock I wasn't yet fully aware of what had transpired (traumatic amnesia). Apparently this was the correct conclusion. With time, details came back to me vividly and they have remained vivid, but God has been extremely gracious in giving me His peace and keeping me from emotional scars.

A few weeks later on November 16, we were notified that the trial would be held the following Wednesday morning, November 24, 1976. Larry had hoped that it would be sufficient for him to go to court in my behalf, but that was not permitted. For it to be a fair trial, we were told that all must be present.

November 24 rolled around and Larry and I were there just before 9:00 a.m., the scheduled time, but on arrival we were informed that the trial had been moved up to between 11:00 and 12:00 because of a staff meeting. So we returned home and waited for them to call. I went back to work in the mission office, and Larry had some things to do on the boat while we were waiting. They called a little after 11:30 a.m. and we immediately returned to the courtroom, but it was around 1:00 or so in the afternoon by the time the trial actually began. When the reason for the delay was explained, we appreciated their thoughtfulness. They had arranged for our case to be the last one tried so they could clear out all the people who had been standing around outside the door to listen to the other trials. They also made ours a "closed door" trial, and also closed the window curtains to block the view of people outside who wanted to watch. I was grateful for these kindnesses.

Incredibly, to the human mind, God lovingly kept me from bitterness and even burdened me to pray for my attacker's spiritual welfare. At the same time, when I thought of seeing him again and going over what had happened, I felt like dissolving into tears.

Going to that trial was one of the most difficult things I'd had to do in a long time. Shirley Rascher accompanied me, and of course Larry was the prime witness. Still running a low grade fever, I felt extremely weak and trembling inside. I asked the Lord to help me trust Him by faith, regardless of how I was feeling. To think of facing that courtroom, especially with my attacker in it, seemed almost too hard to endure but it must be done. I hoped that I would not faint when I came face to face with him.

However, an astounding thing happened when I stepped into the courtroom! I was suddenly possessed of a strength and calmness that could have come only from God. It was almost physical, as if a cloak had been laid around my shoulders. When I looked at Piet, all those fears and terrible feelings were drowned by a feeling of compassion. Seeing him sitting there meekly and all alone, with every-one against him, I couldn't help feeling sorry for him. It hardly seemed possible that this could be the same man who had treated me as he did. They did not allow Larry or me in the courtroom while they heard his statement, but had him stay during mine. He confirmed that everything I stated was true. Then they sent me out and called Larry for questioning.

The trial was on the day before Thanksgiving 1976, but we did not hear the verdict until January 7, 1977. The verdict was guilty and he was sentenced to two years in prison. However, he was allowed to leave the jail every Sunday morning in order to attend church and walked past my apartment, alone, on the way.

Ron and I discussed what course of action I should take in regard to church attendance. Ron told me that my going to a different church would be all right, if the confrontation with Piet in the church that I normally attended would prove too difficult. While I felt sure that no one would criticize my going to a different church, after thinking and praying about it I felt that no one would be edified by it either. Ron agreed that it would be an opportunity for God to manifest His ability to give the grace of forgiveness.

At the church, I tried to give Piet an opportunity to leave without running into me, if he wished to do so. However, instead he went out of his way to come to the front of the church where I was talking with some of the ladies. It was customary for everyone to go around shaking hands with one another after a church service. A few weeks earlier, I might have wondered if I could ever bear for him to touch me again, but when he extended his hand that morning I was able to accept it with the peace of God in my heart.

The low-grade fever that I had contracted before moving to Manokwari, continued with me. I felt extremely and increasingly fatigued, but hoped that it might clear up after treatment for an amebic infection. Instead, It accelerated. At Christmastime I visited Senggo and while there made an appointment with Dr. Dresser, who determined that I had picked up the dreaded "Sentani bug," perhaps on my initial arrival in Sentani. For a year or more I ran a daily fever and lost about 26 pounds. One of the missionaries, Patricia Fillmore, took me home to her mission station in the mountains to rest for a few weeks. Things got better, but as soon as I returned to the office and tried to work the fever returned.

It was decided that medical attention was needed beyond what was available locally, which meant that I would need to leave Irian Jaya for a while. We feared that if I returned to the States the mission might not allow me to return to Irian Jaya, and so we decided to ask if I could go to Australia instead. The international headquarters office in Wheaton gave their approval in a cable received on June 14, 1977:

> *"Office help needed Australia office until October. Suggest Helen Edds go soon if possible accomplishing recuperation and also limited office help then returning Manokwari. We remain hopeful researching cause and cure hepatitis-like disease. Cable response and Wheaton will begin arrangements. - Carl Davis, Far East Secretary"*

I had never been to Australia and did not know anyone there. More changes, new friends, new adventures and more memory-making experiences lay ahead.

AUSTRALIA

Chapter 31

Just a few weeks short of a year after my arrival in Manokwari, on August 2, 1977, I flew to Sentani in preparation for my departure to Sydney, Australia. Another MAF flight was in the air that same day, but that flight did not reach its destination. The plane went down in the mountains, taking with it the lives of pilot Chris Davidson and missionaries Peter and Nel Akse, along with two of their children and their unborn baby.

At the MAF base in Sentani where I stayed that night, the evening's silence was broken by the sound of coffins being made as I went to bed — electric sawing of wood and the pounding of nails. Without a funeral home, these details must be cared for by the missionaries. Some stayed up all night to finish the coffins, and burial took place the next day, with a memorial service held a couple of days later.

Eight days later, August 10, 1977, the day of my departure for Sydney, was another unusual day — and night! My airline ticket reached me shortly before time for takeoff. The plane stopped at Vonimo, Wewak, Madang and Lae. Then we reached Port Moresby. I had been told that I would be overnighting in Port Moresby and that the airline would most likely care for my accommodations, as is customary when an airline's scheduling requires a long wait between connecting flights. A stopover was okay with me, as it would be good to have the trip broken up with a chance to rest between connections. While on the plane, I asked the flight attendant what I should do and she told me to check at the airport desk.

However, on arrival at the Port Moresby airport, no one was at the desk. In fact, the entire terminal was practically empty! *"Lord, what do I do now?"* I prayed. I couldn't haul all my heavy luggage around while looking for help, but neither could I go off and leave it. As I stood at the empty desk, tired and desperately hoping that someone would come, I saw my luggage disappearing out of sight! Quickly retracing my steps across the lobby, I let the workers know that I was there and it was mine. Apparently, not knowing whose luggage it was, they had intended to store it. The employee to whom I had attempted to explain that I needed to leave it in that spot temporarily apparently did not understand a lot of English.

Then another employee, a man in a red tee shirt, appeared. He spoke English fluently and offered to help. He explained that hopefully the airline would someday progress to the point of accommodating passengers who were stuck there due to scheduling, but they were unable to do so at that time. However, he tried to help me find a place to go. He attempted contacting a mission or two and even the American Ambassador, but could not get through to anyone. So there I sat, waiting for what would happen next! I was told that the airport would close at 10:00 p.m.

While the airport employee in the red tee shirt was gone to the telephone, a group of girls, appearing to be teenagers or in their early twenties, drifted into the airport. Out for an evening of joy riding, they saw me – a white woman sitting alone in an almost empty airport – and wondered what I was doing. They came over and began talking with me in fluent English.

After listening to my story, they immediately invited me to go with them and stay in their flat! Boy, was I ever praying for guidance about that as I talked. There I was, a stranger in a strange city, no one knowing where I was, and strangers inviting me to go with them! I didn't want to hurt their feelings if they were genuinely wanting to help; yet it seemed that it could be a dangerous thing to do. Feeling that it wouldn't be a very restful situation either, even if safe, I suggested that we wait and see what the fellow in the red tee shirt came up with before making a decision. It turned out that he never did make contact with anyone.

In discussing the living situation of the girls who invited me to stay with them, I learned that a nonresident could not stay there while the girls were gone to work, and so I would have to go out during the day. We discussed the alternatives of a local guest house, a hostel and different hotels. The girls refused to walk away and leave me in the airport, saying that it was a dangerous city. The airport would be closing in a little while and I would not be permitted to spend the night there. I certainly couldn't spend the night on the street either. They said that there were a lot of killings and rapes at night and that it wasn't safe to be out alone after 5:00 p.m.

Then one of the girls told me that she was a receptionist at a moderately priced hotel – not as expensive as the fancier hotels, nor as inexpensive as a hostel. We finally decided that I would try for a room there. I really didn't want to go with a group of strangers, but it seemed there was no other option. They offered to take me to the hotel and even carried my luggage to their van. Thus I climbed into a vehicle with eleven strangers: ten young women and one young man at the wheel! They situated me in the front seat between the driver and Anne, the hotel receptionist. She told me about the places we were passing, but it was difficult to keep my mind on them.

It seemed a long ride from the airport as the driver sailed along – at one point speeding through a definitely red light. I was really scared, not as much of his driving, as to what I might have let myself in for! Even though they were mostly girls, it would have taken far less than ten of them to overpower me if they intended to rob me and dump me somewhere! As we sped down along, I was telling the Lord that I didn't know whether I should be rejoicing at His abundant provision or worrying that I might have made a foolish mistake in going with these strangers. I wasn't encouraged at all when the driver asked if I didn't know <u>anyone</u> in Port Moresby! Not knowing the area, I had no idea whether we were headed toward the city or away from it.

When we finally pulled up in front of a hotel, my whole being responded with gratitude to God! They refused to let me pay them for the trip. I had no local currency yet, but offered to pay the driver via the receptionist after getting some money exchanged. He insisted that the ride was free. They carried my luggage into the hotel for me and Anne got the key to a room. Then all twelve of us tromped up the stairs to the room, as they carried my luggage. It was not a ritzy place, but seemed very clean and had double locks on the door.

After the whole flock and I were in the room, I told them how I had prayed about my dilemma and how the Lord had used them to answer my prayers. They said that I needed to rest, told me to be sure and lock my door from the inside, and then my eleven angels departed. The next two mornings, August 11 and 12, I had breakfast with Anne at the hotel and saw some of the other girls off and on in my comings and goings during the day.

God's care was abundant! He did not stop with providing a safe place for me to spend the two days in Port Moresby! It turned out that there was a travel bureau next door to the hotel, a bank just up the street and a post office about a block in the other direction. One of the girls worked at the travel bureau! She introduced me to a lady there who answered all my questions regarding onward travel and other needs, confirmed my onward flight and gave information on how to contact the airport bus. Three of the girls worked at the bank, two of them in the area where I needed to exchange travelers checks! They saw me coming from the post office and walked with me to the bank. I stopped at the telephone office to phone the TEAM Center in Sydney and tell them where I was and when I'd be arriving.

Checkout time at the hotel was 10:00 a.m. On Friday morning, as I sat on the front porch of the hotel and waited for my airport ride to arrive, Anne was there. I said goodbye and thanked her again for all her help.

We landed in Sydney during a rain, their first in six weeks we were told. They asked us to cover our faces while they sprayed the cabin in which we were sitting, before we were allowed to get off the plane. This was to prevent any harmful insects that might have accompanied us on the flight from New Guinea from entering Australia.

Not knowing anyone in Australia and not knowing who would meet me, I progressed through immigration and customs and entered the waiting room. A pleasant looking young woman approached me, introduced herself and asked if my name was Helen. Her name was Phyllis Woodhouse. Phyllis took me to the TEAM Center, made some tea and toast and visited with me for a while. The TEAM Center was located in Homebush, a Sydney suburb, in a red brick house, the back part of which had been converted into offices. There were some bedrooms, a bath, kitchen and dining/meeting room in the remainder of the house.

Phyllis left a little after 9:00 p.m. While awaiting

the return of Jenny and Graeme Thitchener, the young couple who served as host and hostess at the center, I read the mail that had accumulated for me. Then, being very tired and sleepy, I finally decided to give it up and go to bed around 11:00 p.m. Just as I turned out the light, Jenny and Graeme arrived and I got up and went to introduce myself to them.

The following two nights, Saturday and Sunday, Bill Thitchener, the Australian Director, and his wife Noelean, took me with them to a missionary convention. Both were late nights by the time I got to bed (midnight or after). On Monday I tried to help in the office and also prepared to speak at the Monday night prayer meeting. After the Monday night meeting, Noelean stayed to show me some of the office routine and that took us until almost 10:30 p.m. Life was much busier than I expected. There had apparently been a communication mixup between the TEAM office in Wheaton and the TEAM office in Sydney. I had come to Australia to recuperate and to give limited help in the office. But the Australian staff was under the impression that I had come to carry a normal load. It was difficult to know how to handle the situation. Always wanting to do my share and not wanting to disappoint them, but knowing that I was much weaker than they realized, I was much in prayer about it.

Tuesday, the fourth day after my arrival, I was again seeking to help in the office and managed to get through the morning. I was awfully tired by noon and thought I'd rest immediately after lunch and go to bed early that evening. However, right after lunch something urgent came up in the office and I had to go back and try to help. By late afternoon, I knew it was more than fatigue, as I began to feel feverish. More and more miserable as the night went on, I felt chills starting and fever rising, accompanied by a deepening backache, headache and nausea. By morning I was very weak and a doctor was called to come to the house to see me.

A short time later, I moved to a comfortable little house that had been loaned to TEAM by a couple who was traveling out of the country for six months or so. I enjoyed staying there and commuted to the TEAM office daily by bus. The months rolled by. I continued unwell but attempted to help in the office as much as possible. Joan Mellor, a Canadian member of TEAM who had served in Chad, was scheduled to arrive in November and take over the office work, and we all looked forward to her coming. On November 10, 1977, Bill Thitchener picked me up at the house where I was staying and took me with him to meet Joan at the airport. After a busy day and evening, it was around midnight when Joan and I got home to the house we would be sharing temporarily and went to bed.

The next morning, I awoke tired but got up and fixed breakfast. Then during breakfast, I began feeling almost too tired to sit up and started experiencing hard chills, a high fever, vomiting and extreme weakness. Joan phoned the doctor and he said he would send an ambulance for me. It was like heaven when the ambulance staff arrived, carefully picked me up, put me in the ambulance and took me to a hospital bed! Joan's first view of Sydney was from the front seat of that ambulance! I was diagnosed with a severe case of malaria. The doctor told me later that he didn't go to bed that night until he knew that I was going to be all right. He felt that another attack of malaria as severe as the one I just experienced could easily be fatal.

Two more very special people that God brought into my life in Australia were Colin and Enid Shedden. Both were committed Christians, who were burdened for missions. For that reason, Enid had come to work in the TEAM office. They helped me in so many ways. When I was discharged from the hospital on November 15, they took me into their home and took wonderful care of me until I returned to the TEAM Center on November 22. That day I went to the doctor for a checkup and he scheduled a liver scan for the following day, followed by an intravenous pyelogram on November 24. I was admitted back to the hospital for a liver biopsy on November 25 and discharged from the hospital again on November 26.

In early December, the doctor recommended that I not return to Irian Jaya, but said that if I did I should wait at least three more months. We shared this information with the home office back in Wheaton and received a cable from Carl Davis, the Far East Secretary, approving my continuing in Australia for three more months. That meant I would spend Christmas in Australia.

Another special friend was a dear little white-haired Australian lady, who volunteered her time at the TEAM Center, Pearl Klix. Pearl had been a big help to me when I was so ill at the Center, and she invited me to go home with her for Christmas. During the holidays, she and some friends took me to a beautiful Christmas program at the famed Sydney Opera House. On Christmas Day, Pearl fixed a wonderful Australian style meal for me with leg of lamb as the main course, and she took me with her to a Christmas service at her church.

After receiving my latest medical report in March, Carl Davis phoned from the Wheaton office on March 30, 1978, asking me to return to the USA.

During my stay in Sydney, Phyllis Woodhouse who had met me on my arrival in Sydney and befriended me in numerous ways, sensed that God was leading her to go to Irian Jaya for a short term ministry. She took me to the airport on April 17, 1978, for the flight that would return me to the USA. As we sat in her car discussing her upcoming trip to Irian Jaya, she smiled and said, *"This is all your fault!"* That was an encouraging word with which to depart and to continue my journey into whatever God had ahead. I could not go back, but God was sending someone else to help.

AMERICA

Chapter 32

My journey with God which had taken me around the world more than once had brought me back to America. I landed at Chicago's O'Hare Airport on April 18, 1978, and was met by Carl and Agnes Davis, Sylvia Fuller and Jay Lake from the TEAM office. The ensuing years would be filled with many more challenges and opportunities to experience His guidance and grace. A verse that kept coming to mind as time went on was in Hebrews 13:14 *"For here have we no continuing city . . ."* I could certainly relate to that!

The next eight years found me at the home office of the mission. In the beginning, there was the familiar quandary. Try to return to Irian Jaya? Serve in some other country? Or continue at the international headquarters office? There were needs and opportunities in the international office and doctors had discouraged my returning overseas. An assignment to the home staff seemed the correct choice.

By the spring of 1980, two things were on the horizon: 1) I was to make a decision by April concerning whether to continue in the office indefinitely or consider serving in some other country, and 2) there was the possibility that medical clearance would be granted at my April checkup, which could point to a return to Irian Jaya.

Two days before my medical checkup in April, the serious automobile accident of a coworker, Doris Frazer, plunged me into new responsibilities. Then, at the checkup, complete medical clearance was not given. These two happenings converged to show me that I should continue in the work at the international headquarters. As Doris's recovery stretched into more than six months, spanning the busiest time of the year for our department, life became full of pressures and inescapable responsibilities.

In September 1980 I managed to take off time to drive home to Arkansas for a few days and to bring my parents back to Wheaton for a visit in the cooler climate. They had experienced a dreadfully hot summer in Arkansas that year. Less than twenty-four hours after our arrival in Wheaton, my 94 year old stepfather fell in my apartment, fractured his hip, and was rushed to a local hospital by paramedics. The following morning he had surgery and then developed pneumonia, but after several days he began to improve. Each night after work and on weekends, my mother and I went to the hospital and later to the nursing home where he was recuperating. By the latter part of October we were able to return him to Arkansas by air – his very first flight! He seemed to thoroughly enjoy the trip, including the delicious meal that was served aboard the plane.

In late October, Doris Frazer was able to return to the office part-time and I began the transition into another position. By the end of November she was working full time and I moved more completely into a new work of assisting Nelson Bezanson with summer workers and short term missionaries.

At Christmas time I flew back to Arkansas for a few days, and shortly after my arrival there, my step-father developed pneumonia, becoming critically ill. On his and my mother's thirty-sixth wedding anniversary, December 28, 1980, he was admitted to the hospital, where he passed away on January 2, 1981 at the age of 95.

In July 1982, I was offered the opportunity of becoming the coordinator for TEAM's summer and special short term programs, as Nelson Bezanson with whom I had been working was transferring to a TEAM office in Canada. TEAM's summer program was for young adults, usually college students, who had completed at least two years of Bible school or college. They were given assignments to assist in the work in various countries during the summer months and an opportunity to learn from career missionaries. The Special Short Term Program was for adults of all ages with maturity and experience, ranging from young professionals to retirees, who volunteered to meet specific temporary needs. A physician or surgeon could replace a missionary doctor during his furlough. A school teacher could teach missionary children for an entire school year. Nurses could pitch in from several months to a year. Others could help as secretaries, bookkeepers, construction workers and maintenance personnel.

September 1, 1982, was my first official day in that position, one which I enjoyed very much. It involved a lot of correspondence and telephone conversations, screening of applicants, overseeing visa applications, travel arrangements, finances, orientation and debriefing of workers along with a variety of other matters.

Interspersed with the work in the home office were missionary conferences, trips to California and New York relative to orientation for summer workers, and many personal experiences apart from the office.

Then in 1986 once again I stood at the threshold of a new chapter in my life. There were many unknowns, but one thing was certain: God held my hand and for that I was deeply grateful. It was good to know that my hand was securely in His as new ventures were about to unfold.

The early dawn of October 31, 1986, found my little brown Plymouth Horizon loaded to the hilt in the driveway outside my West Chicago, IL, apartment. I was on my way back to Arkansas. Although most of my possessions had been eliminated in preparation for the move, still the little car was filled to the brim: a desk, two folding bookcases, a small TV, a couple of large rugs, clothing, boxes, bags, Mitzi, Mo (my two cats), a litter box and me! After a two-day trip, with smoke billowing from beneath the hood of the car, we pulled in at my mother's house.

This move was one that I had never expected, a return to my home town. I thought that I would always be with TEAM, either in the United States or overseas, and the Chicago area became home to me. I had lived away from Arkansas longer than I lived there before leaving. However, as I considered my mother's situation — widowed, living alone and not well, I sensed God's leading to help her. I felt that God was speaking to me specifically through some verses in the Bible in 1 Timothy, chapter 5, especially verses 4, 8 and 16.

> *Verse 4: But if any widow have children or nephews, let them learn first to shew piety at home, and to requite their parents: for that is good and acceptable before God.*
>
> *Verse 8: But if any provide not for his own, and specially for those of his own house, he hath denied the faith, and is worse than an infidel.*
>
> *Verse 16: If any woman that believeth have widows, let her relieve them . . .*

I settled into life with my mother in her two bedroom house and faced the next task: finding a job. Job hunting was a new, educational and interesting experience. Employment was necessary in order to support myself and to help with our combined living expenses. I realized that I could not expect an administrative type position such as I had with TEAM in directing the summer and short term programs, since I did not know that much about any local organization. Nor could I enter the field of nursing. Thinking that I would never need it again in this country I had allowed my nursing license to lapse years before. I still had an Indonesian license, but that was of no value in the United States. Also, since I had been out of medical work for so long, I wouldn't have felt comfortable trying to enter that field without returning to school first. I needed immediate income from employment, and so could not take time out to go back to school. I accepted a receptionist position in a local clinic, where I worked for almost three and a half years. Later I found work as a neurodiagnostic transcriptionist in another clinic, and worked there for over seven years. God brought some wonderful people and varied experiences into my life through both of these opportunities.

My mother loved to garden, but hadn't been up to gardening for several years. So my first spring there, together we planted a small garden in the back yard. My mother called it our "postage stamp garden" because it was so small, but — thanks to her touch — it produced prolifically! We enjoyed fresh lettuce, green onions, yellow squash, and cucumbers. The cucumber vines grew so well that they climbed a tree and we had cucumbers hanging from the tree! We were also delighted with an abundance of tomatoes, sweet peppers and hot peppers, as well as cantaloupes and okra, in addition to getting some flower beds under way.

Since she was alone during the day while I worked at the clinic, my mother and I spent our evenings and week ends doing things like grocery shopping, working in the yard, just being together and of course attending church. In earlier years my mother had been a meticulous housekeeper and though congestive heart failure was weakening her and her eyesight was failing, she continued to do an adequate job of it. When I tried to help by getting into deeper cleaning on Saturdays, my day off from the clinic, she'd say *"Let's don't spend all our time cleaning. Let's do things while we can and enjoy the time we have together."*

We began to make plans to travel. She wanted to see the ocean again, and we talked of moving to Florida. We thought that perhaps when I had worked at the clinic long enough to earn a vacation we would make a trip there. If I could find a job, we would return to Arkansas, sell the house and move to Florida. We would get away from the cold winters and be near the seashore we both loved. But that was not to be. As my mom realized that she was getting weaker and perhaps could not travel that far, she decided that she'd like to visit Branson, Missouri, a popular tourist area not too far from home. I had never been there. My dream had been to take her to Hawaii someday, but neither time nor finances ever permitted that.

Before we traveled anywhere, she was called to her heavenly home. We had about sixteen months together. Though she had not been in the best of health for several years, the suddenness of her home-going still came as a shock. She was in church on Sunday, cooked dinner on Monday, went into the hospital on Tuesday and passed away on Thursday, February 25, 1988.

Spring was my mom's favorite season. As soon as Christmas was past, she began looking forward to it. We thrilled at the sight of each year's first blossoms, whether together or by letter or telephone. That year, our first bright yellow jonquil burst into full bloom while I was attending her funeral. Returning home and observing it, my heart ached that this time we could not share it.

But the Lord reminded me that the beauty of spring on earth cannot begin to compare with the beauty she was experiencing in heaven. Nor could the places that I had planned to take her begin to measure up to the wonders she was seeing there. Her funeral service was held at the church, as she had requested. It was a lovely day and a lovely service. The skies were blue and the sun was shining brightly with a record-breaking February 27 temperature of 79 degrees. As I sat in the cemetery looking at the beautiful flowers against the blue of the sky, my thoughts turned to the resurrection.

After my mom went to be with the Lord early in 1988, I thought it was likely that He would move me back into full-time Christian work. But circumstances and responsibilities kept me in my home town in Arkansas. I sometimes wondered if God had put me on the shelf and at other times whether people questioned why I was not more involved in "full time" Christian work. But God had work to do in my own heart and He gave opportunities for ministry there, as I met spiritually hungry people in many places. He helped me realize that what He desires is faithfulness; I must leave to Him what anyone else thought about what I was doing or not doing.

My Aunt Hazel, my mother's youngest sister and only remaining sibling, also lived alone in Fort Smith, and as time went on she needed more and more assistance. In the beginning it usually involved only a couple of nights a week, things like checking on her and taking her grocery shopping, and then transporting her to appointments and so forth. When she could no longer go shopping, even with my assistance, she gave me her list and I did her shopping for her. Before long she also needed help with duties like bill paying, correspondence and laundry. But she persisted in doing her best to remain ambulatory. After getting off work at the clinic, I cooked her meals at my house, took them to her apartment and then helped her exercise by walking up and down the hallway of the apartment building to maintain her strength. Sometimes we stopped off and visited a neighbor in a nearby apartment. Other times, on a sunny day, I took her outside in a wheel chair so that we could look at the flowers and birds and sit in the gazebo on the lawn for a few minutes. Before going home in the evenings, I set up her medications for the next day and placed her breakfast items of cereal and instant coffee on the kitchen table for the next morning.

During the daytime, a home health care worker came to the apartment and helped her with her bath while I was at work. I thought of moving her to my home, but decided that it was safer for her to stay in her apartment. If she moved in with me she would be alone all day while I was working. In her apartment she had neighbors nearby and also a call switch in her bedroom and bathroom in case she needed to contact the apartment desk for help.

By the beginning of 1995 she needed help every day, literally seven days a week, including Saturdays, Sundays and holidays. I was "on call" twenty-four hours a day. She was a wonderful lady and I loved her very much. Even so, between working full time and being involved so completely in her life in addition to my other responsibilities, 1995 is seen as a year of constant exhaustion. Nevertheless, I was glad that I could help her and felt that it was a ministry God had given to me.

As her health continued to deteriorate and she could no longer do even such simple things as turning herself over in bed, it was necessary for her to enter a nursing home. Her swallowing reflex was gone and she was placed on tube feeding. She also required oxygen all the time. But I knew that she counted on my continuing daily visits, often twice on Saturday and twice on Sunday, and I continued to care for her basic personal needs. Life had grown very difficult for her and for me.

In April 1997, I wrote to Lorene,

> *"For a long time it seems as if I have been on the back side of the desert. Sometimes I feel that God has something else ahead. Other times I wonder if the remainder of my life, whether it is short or long, will be carried out in continuing here and/or if and when He leads on, how He will work out all the "hurdles" that now exist. Yet I know that*

He has been faithful in the past, and that whatever the future holds, His perfect will is all I want. I have failed Him many times, especially during the difficult years here, but I praise Him for what He is doing in me. Please pray that I will be faithful and will trust and obey – whatever. Thanks!"

We do not always understand why things happen as they do. God's ways are higher than our ways and His understanding infinitely greater than ours. But both my aunt and I, along with her daughter Alice who had moved back home from out of state to be near her mother, understood that God loved us and that – regardless of how things appeared – He had our best interests at heart. My aunt's favorite verse was Romans 8:28,

"For we know that all things work together for good for those who love Him . . ."

Life's hectic pace seemed to reach a crescendo at the end of 1997 and the beginning of 1998. My aunt was in and out of the hospital and I continued to work full time at the clinic to support myself. Physical exhaustion reached a peak, but there seemed no way to stop.

Along with these things, winter came to Arkansas and the heating system in my house quit working. My cat Mitzi, who had been with me for seventeen years, died. My brother Tom came from Florida for his first Christmas with us in many years. He was widowed, but had always felt the need to be at home in Florida for his adult children. That year, however, as no one was coming home, he decided to come north and celebrate the holidays with us. Then, shortly after his arrival my sister was rushed to the hospital. In February my aunt was back in the hospital. In fact, another aunt was also in the hospital at the same time.

On February 13, 1998, God released my Aunt Hazel from her tired body and took her Home into His glorious presence. Her earthly journey had been completed; mine would continue.

BOB

Chapter 33

God's faithfulness does not fail. He is with us, watching over us, even when everything appears otherwise. Sometimes things seem so dark and then it is as if God says, "*It is enough!*" In a flash things change. He parts the clouds and sets us on a new path. Other times, for reasons known to Him, difficulties continue and He lovingly gives grace. Either way, He can be trusted!

My darkness seemed so dark and my body so tired. Then as if turning a corner, life took on a new dimension as God unexpectedly and graciously sent a new source of encouragement into my life. His name was Robert Rhodes Frazier. Bob was a friend, a missionary with TEAM and a former coworker in Irian Jaya. He could understand my fatigue, my being stretched to the limit, as he, too, had been through an extended period of care giving. He had faithfully cared for his beloved wife Doris through a fourteen-year illness, as she battled with Alzheimer's

Disease. The Lord had called her Home during the past year.

Bob and I first met in Chicago in 1961, when I was twenty-six and he was thirty-three. I had just completed college. Bob and Doris had recently completed their first term of missionary service. They served with TEAM in Irian Jaya and Bob was serving as instructor for the Irian Jaya group of candidates at TEAM's Candidate School that summer. I joined the group of aspiring missionaries interested in Irian Jaya and drank in every word that Bob and Doris shared with us. Then I became better acquainted with them after going to Irian Jaya, where we served on the south coast among the same tribal group, the Asmat. Though we worked on different mission stations, occasionally I passed through Yaosakor where they lived. However, after I was transferred to the north coast and the work in Manokwari, and later still went to Australia and then back to the Chicago area, we lost contact for a number of years. Bob and Doris moved to Florida to represent TEAM, when they were detained at home by Doris's health. They later began a church in their home, which is now the South Babcock Street Baptist Church in Palm Bay, Florida.

Bob took care of Doris at home for about four years, but eventually her condition worsened so much that it was necessary to admit her to a nursing home. She was there almost ten years and then the Lord called her Home to heaven.

Several months after Doris's death, Bob came across my e-mail address and decided to write to me.

It was good to hear from him, especially since I felt that he could genuinely understand my situation. Missionaries are like a family and we feel close to each other, so here was someone with whom I could relate in many ways. We had worked with the same mission in the same country, with the same tribal group, spoke the same foreign language, and had even attended the same school in California (Biola School of Missionary Medicine) — seven years apart. Bob's e-mail letters brightened my dark days like rays of sunlight, as we discussed everything from theology to music, likes/dislikes, funny stories out of our past and, of course, shared prayer requests. Eventually cards, letters and phone conversations were added to our daily e-mail communications.

Bob was born in Durham, North Carolina, on December 18, 1927, the son of a tobacco farmer. At the age of ten, he was baptized in a local Baptist church, but later in life he said, " . . . *it was only a profession – not the real thing."*

During World War II, the North Carolina property which had been the Frazier farm became part of a large military training camp and the family moved to a new location. After high school graduation, Bob's interest in photography led him to enroll in the New York Institute of Photography in New York City. But that aspiration was short lived when Uncle Sam sent word that he was to report to Fort Bragg, North Carolina, for induction into the United States Army. He was sent to Fort Belvoir, Virginia, for basic training, after which he remained there in a school to learn photolithography (map making). He expected to go to Tokyo, Japan, from there, along with his school unit, an exciting prospect for a nineteen-year-old who had not seen much of the world outside his home area of North Carolina. Once again, however, plans for his immediate future were curtailed when he developed a severe nosebleed three days before the unit was to sail from Camp Stoneman, California. Doctors felt he should not sail with the unit. Disappointment, bitterness and fright overtook him at the prospect of starting over and making new friends.

Bob's new assignment was to an outfit in Fort Lewis Washington. The following is his story, as told in his book, "Our Passionate Journey."

> *Shortly after arriving, I noticed some of the fellows in the barracks were always talking about God. They even knelt to pray before getting into their bunks at night. They always had a Bible with them which they read at every opportunity.*
>
> *This seemed very weird to me. I had never seen anyone quite so "religious," not even the preachers I had known. Though reared in a Christian home with very spiritual grandparents, I had not been led toward a personal relationship with Christ.*
>
> *One time, in Washington, D.C., while I was eating a sandwich in the Salvation Army Center, a fellow came to my table and began to "cram" his religion down my throat. I almost choked on my sandwich!*
>
> *But these fellows were different. One*

Saturday night they asked me to go to church with them the next day. Feeling that I too was a "religious" person, I agreed to meet them at their church. I failed to keep my promise, however. Instead, I went to a movie. When that one was over, I went to another.

It was late when I left the last theater, so I proceeded towards the bus station to return to base. God had something else in mind, however. Just 'happening' to walk past the church that I was supposed to have attended, I could hear enthusiastic singing. I was irresistibly drawn inside.

Sitting on the back pew, I saw people waving their arms in the air as they sang. Many of them were shouting, 'Praise the Lord, glory, Hallelujah!' That frightened me. What in the world had I gotten myself into?

When they finally stopped singing and the preaching began, something happened to me that I can't explain. Bible words began to come alive for me. The preacher kept pointing his finger at me. 'Be not deceived, God is not mocked, whatsoever a man soweth, that shall he also reap!'

I realized that I had been mocking God. A vision of Christ hanging on a cross came between me and the preacher. Then it dawned on me: Jesus was hanging there for me! I too felt like shouting, "Glory, hallelujah. He died for me. I deserve to be there but He took my place!"

At the invitation I ran to the altar. Falling on my knees I wept tears of remorse for my rebellious attitude towards God. I asked Him to forgive me. The preacher came down and asked me if I was saved. I told him I didn't know what he meant. He then asked me if I had confessed my sins and asked Jesus into my heart. 'Yes,' I answered. He then shouted to the whole church that this young soldier was 'saved!'

At that moment a small black woman in a long, faded red dress jumped up from the front row. She ran directly to me, throwing her arms around my neck, shouting and praising the Lord. This was March 16, 1947, before integration. My face turned a deep red. It was two days before I discovered she was totally blind! My color did not matter. A child of God was born! God called me to preach a few days later.

After his discharge from military service in October of that year, Bob enrolled in a small Bible school in New York State. Then in the fall of 1949 he transferred to Bob Jones University in Greenville, South Carolina. It was there that he met Doris, who was also a student. She was from Pennsylvania. They were both burdened for the land of India and wanted to go there as missionaries. To their great disappointment, they were unable to obtain visas for that land. God led them to serve in New Guinea instead.

Now, in 1998, with twenty-eight years of

missionary service behind him and with his wife in Heaven, Bob was at another crossroad in his life. He was seeking God's guidance for the future, as was I. In God's wise and wonderful ways, He was causing our journeys to converge.

As Bob and I talked with each other every day by e-mail and then by phone calls, cards and letters, we were *really* getting to know each other. We had been acquaintances/friends for many years, but we had not known each other at the level we were reaching now. Previously he had been a fellow missionary and friend, but somewhere along the way during 1998 our friendship grew deeper and turned into love. Bob said that he knew where the relationship was going before I did! And he was right! I had thought that even if he was interested in me, there was no way we could ever get together. He lived in Florida and I lived in Arkansas, over a thousand miles apart!

With one of the cards that he sent to me, Bob enclosed some snapshots of his house. I wasn't quite sure why he sent photos of his house, but since he appeared to have an interest in houses I told him that I would send him a picture of mine.

He wrote that when I came to visit my brother, who lived less than an hour's drive from him, he would like to take me out to dinner. I thanked him, but explained that my brother always came to my home town to visit and so I did not come to Florida.

The Saturday before Easter in April, 1998, I returned home I found a florist's note saying that they had attempted a delivery. Surprised, I wondered who could be sending me flowers. Perhaps it was someone who had just learned about my aunt's passing away a couple of months earlier and wanted to send something, I thought. What a surprise when, after I called the florist to let them know I was home, they delivered a lovely orchid corsage! Inside was a note from Bob, saying *"Happy Resurrection Day!"* My heart was stirred by this very unexpected gift.

About ten days later during the course of our regular e-mail on April 21, I shared a serious prayer request with Bob. Now that both my mother and aunt were in heaven, I was praying about what to do next. I had been contacted by a Christian university about an opportunity in coordinating one of their ministries. I was not able to consider it at the time they contacted me, as they needed someone sooner than I could have gotten there. However, they might have other opportunities available.

The following day, Bob wrote,

> *Your letter of last night has left me in a quandary. . . I hope you will not make any decisions too soon regarding a future ministry.*
>
> *I really wish I could sit down and talk with you for a few hours. I feel that we have so much in common that we really understand each other . . .*
>
> *I hope the tone of this letter is not coming as a surprise to you . . . Please forgive me if I sound too forward and blunt. I just want you to know where I am.*
>
> *I am not just looking for someone to fill a void in my life, but rather am seeking God's*

will . . . It's difficult to say that one loves someone whom they have not seen for over twenty-six years, yet my gut feeling is that there is a spark there that needs to be blown into a flame.

I wrote back,

Dear Bob,

Thank you for your precious letter. I am so honored and blessed by what you have written.

This will just be a short note for now, but I want to at least let you know that I have received your letter, that I have already been on my knees laying it before the Lord, and that I will try to write more tomorrow.

I think I have felt more free to share my heart with you than with any man I have ever known . . . But I have also felt that I must be careful not to read more into our growing friendship than you intended. So I do thank you for being open with me.

What I want, too, is God's perfect will. Let's keep seeking that, with the confidence that He will confirm His leading and that He will provide all that is needed to accomplish it.

Our past ministries had been completed, and both of us were beginning to realize that God was leading us into a new life and to serve Him together.

In June, 1998, in God's wonderful plan, we had an opportunity to overcome the many miles that separated us. I went to Tennessee to participate in the reaffirmation of wedding vows of two dear friends, Lorene and Bill Overway, on the occasion of their thirtieth wedding anniversary. At the same time, Bob was in the midst of a two-month tour of speaking engagements across the United States. It worked out that he had a few days free between meetings during the very same time that I would be in Tennessee. We decided to meet in Nashville and spend some time together. From the start we felt so comfortable and at ease with one another as we discussed important issues and prayed together.

The second night in Tennessee, I was hit with an upset stomach! Bob had some lovely romantic outings planned, but I was too ill to go on most of them. As we sat across from each other at breakfast in a restaurant the next morning while I tried to consume my tea and toast, Bob looked at me and said, "I love you." I felt that I must look very unlovable to anyone at that moment!

On Wednesday evening, June 24, Bob took me out for dinner. Because of my nausea I only ate some Jello, but even that would not stay down. I had to run to the Ladies Room and throw up before leaving the restaurant! After that I felt much better for a few hours and during that time, as we sat in his car and talked, Bob asked me to marry him. I gladly said yes! I also said, "*Are you sure you still want me after all this!*" He kissed me for the first time. We decided that in days to come we would laugh about the night he asked me to marry him and I threw up!

After many difficult years for both of us, we

were overwhelmed with the love and joy with which God was blessing us and flooding our hearts. When Bob took me into his arms, I felt safe, secure and at peace. I had not anticipated such joy before reaching heaven!

We chose to have a quiet wedding at the home of former Irian Jaya coworkers, Chuck and Bernita Preston, in Topeka, KS. Chuck performed the ceremony for us on September 26, 1998. Bob's son Steve, who lived nearby in Missouri, sang and served as best man. Lorene was my matron of honor and her husband Bill escorted me and gave me to Bob with their blessing.

Our lives have been full of travels around the world and the joining of our lives also included many places: we met in Chicago, worked in Irian Jaya, became engaged in Tennessee, married in Kansas, honeymooned in Missouri, and then Bob moved me from Arkansas to Florida.

God is true to His Word. He keeps His promises. He said,

> *"Have not **I** commanded thee? Be strong and of a good courage; be not afraid, neither be thou dismayed; for the Lord they God is with thee whithersoever thou goest."* Joshua 1:9

When He impressed that message on my youthful heart I had no idea of all it would involve. But he has been with me as He promised. The final destination will be reached when I am Home with Him

Who has led, sustained, taught and blessed me all these years. Until then, the journey continues.

Lead on, O King Eternal,
We follow, not with fears;
For gladness breaks like morning
Where'er Thy face appears.

Thy cross is lifted o'er us,
We journey in its light;
The crown awaits the conquest;
Lead on, O God of might!

Printed in the United States
22361LVS00001BA/10-51